JOE GATTO

Sails, Swords, and Smugglers

A Swashbuckling Journey into Colonial America's Pirate Underworld

Contents

Prologue: A Treasure Chest of Lessons and Understanding

Imagine opening a dusty old chest hidden in your attic. It's full of mysterious items, each one telling a story from a time long ago. Studying history is like opening that treasure chest; the past unfolds, rich with stories, lessons, and insights about our world.

Why should we study history? It might seem irrelevant to some, as it talks about a time that we did not witness or live in. But, you see, history is like a time machine. It transports us back in time, helps us understand our ancestors' actions, and offers us lessons that remain valuable today. It paints a picture of where we came from, how we've evolved, and can even provide clues about where we might be headed.

Just like detectives, historians critically analyze events, people, and places from the past. When we read history, we must become detectives too! Every source, every document, every story must be questioned. Who wrote it? Why did they write it? What was their perspective? How might things look different from another point of view? This is the critical reading that history teaches us, and it's a skill that's important in all aspects of life.

By reading critically, we can discern between fact and opinion, assess different viewpoints, and learn to respect diversity. It can also guide us in making connections to the present day. History does not exist in a vacuum; it is intimately tied to our current world. The struggles for justice in the past have shaped our laws today. The revolutions of yesterday influenced our governments today. The inventions, the wars, the movements – they have all left a mark on our modern society.

Remember, history is not just about memorizing dates and names. Instead, when you read about an event, ask yourself: "How did this event shape the society and culture at that time? Why did people think it was okay to do things that we know are not okay today? What impacts did it have on ordinary people's lives? How does this event connect with what I see in the world around me today?" Asking these questions deepens your understanding and makes history come alive!

Now, why is knowing history beneficial for young people like you? One of the primary reasons is it helps to cultivate a sense of identity and belonging. By understanding the history of your country, you're learning about your roots. It provides context for how your community and country have evolved over the years, and it might even help explain some of your family traditions.

Studying world history broadens this understanding even more. It introduces us to different cultures, religions, traditions, and perspectives. It fosters empathy, understanding, and respect for other cultures, which is essential in our increasingly connected world.

Furthermore, history is full of stories of human achievements, failures, courage, and determination. These stories inspire us. They show us that change is possible and that one person can indeed make a difference. They teach us that progress takes time, and that while we may face challenges, our collective efforts can lead to a better future.

So, jump into the treasure chest of history! Discover the wonders of ancient civilizations, the courage of great leaders, the transformation brought by revolutions, and the lessons from our past mistakes. Remember to read critically, connect the past to the present, and most importantly, enjoy the journey! For in studying history, we're not just learning about the past, we're preparing for the future.

History: Opening Doors to Imagination and Understanding

Imagine a time machine transporting us back to a different era, or a magical book with pages turning into portals to the past. Sounds like an exciting movie or an enchanting novel, right? But here's a little secret – history can do just that!

Often, we might think of history as a pile of boring facts and dates. In reality, however, history is much more. It's an infinite collection of stories, a treasure trove of human experiences, and an endless source of inspiration that can fuel our imagination.

When we delve into history, we don't just learn about what happened – we witness the triumphs and trials of the human spirit, the rise and fall of civilizations, and the birth of ideas that have changed our world. Reading about the adventures of explorers, the battles of knights, the discoveries of scientists, or the struggles of revolutionaries can be just as engaging as any fantasy novel. In fact, it can be even more captivating because these stories really happened!

As we immerse ourselves in these stories, we're doing more than just reading – we're imagining. We picture the pirate ships of the 1700s or what life was like in colonial Boston. We envision how it might have felt to discover a new land or invent a groundbreaking technology.

By stimulating our imagination in this way, history can make us more creative thinkers. At the end of this book there are creative writing prompts to help you write your own pirate stories after imagining what the real stories must have really been like. It opens our minds to new ideas, perspectives, and possibilities.

So as you read, try to imagine the sights, sounds, and smells of pirate ships, sea battles, and colonial American cities. In addition, when you see a word or phrase you don't understand, keep reading and try to understand its meaning through context. If you still don't understand it; look it up in a dictionary or Google.

Not only that, but history gives our imagination a grounding in reality. When we learn about the past, we gain a better understanding of why the world is the way it is today. We can see the sequence of cause and effect that has led to our present circumstances. This understanding can inspire us to imagine and create a better future. It can empower us to become active participants in our world, equipped with the knowledge of what has worked or failed before.

Moreover, studying history helps us realize that the world has not always been as we know it. Cultures, technologies, and societies have changed dramatically over time. This can inspire us to dream about what changes might come in the future. After all, if humankind could evolve from living in caves to exploring outer space, what else could we achieve?

In a nutshell, history is not just about the past – it's a gateway to understanding the present and imagining the future. It allows us to dream and to connect those dreams to the real world. So, don't just read history – live it, feel it, imagine it! Who knows, you might be the one making history someday...

Introduction

Prepare to set sail on a thrilling adventure back in time, to a world filled with daring pirates, secretive smugglers, and exciting tales of the high seas. Welcome to "Sails, Swords, and Smugglers: A Swashbuckling Journey into Colonial America's Pirate Underworld". We are about to journey from the year 1650 to 1780, a time when pirates roamed the oceans and smugglers snuck precious goods across borders.

Before we start our adventure, let's make sure we understand two important words: piracy and smuggling.

Pirates, you've probably heard of them. But who were they really? Pirates were seafaring robbers, outlaws of the ocean who sailed under their own flag. They attacked other ships, stealing their cargo, and sometimes even the ship itself. And, believe it or not, pirates didn't just exist in storybooks and movies; they were real people who lived and worked during this exciting time.

While the life of a pirate may seem full of thrilling adventures and camaraderie, it's important to remember that they were, in essence, criminals of the high seas. Pirates often led violent and dangerous lives, full of hardships and uncertainties. They stole from others, often using force and intimidation, and were responsible for numerous acts of destruction and loss of life. Many lived in constant fear of being captured and facing severe punishments, which, in many cases, meant hanging. Life at sea was also incredibly harsh, with pirates facing deadly diseases, injuries from battles, and often poor living conditions. Despite the romanticized image often depicted in stories and films, the reality of a pirate's life was far from glamorous. It was a life chosen out of desperation, rebellion, or a desire for independence from societal norms, but it often came with heavy costs.

Smuggling may not seem as dramatic as piracy, but it was just as sneaky and can be just as thrilling. Smugglers were people who moved goods from one place to another, without permission. This was usually because the goods were valuable, like gold or spices, and the people in power wanted to tax them. So, instead of paying those taxes, smugglers would sneak the goods around, often at night and in secret places.

Now that we know what pirates and smugglers were, let's talk about where and when we'll be exploring. Our journey will take us from bustling ports in Europe, through the sunny islands of the Caribbean, along the dangerous coastlines of Africa, and finally, to the new and growing colonies in America. Each of these places was a critical piece of our puzzle, a part of the wild and wonderful world of pirates and smugglers in the colonial era.

In Europe, mighty kingdoms like England, France, and Spain sent ships across the seas, filled with goods to trade and hungry for the wealth of new lands. The Caribbean, with its turquoise waters and tropical islands, was a favorite hiding place for pirates and a busy hub for smugglers. Africa, with its diverse cultures and rich resources, became a reluctant player in this dangerous game. And the American colonies, young and growing, were often the targets of pirate attacks and the final destination for smuggled goods.

So, grab your compass and your courage as we prepare to embark on a swashbuckling journey back in time. Keep your eyes open, your wits about you, and hold on tight, because it's going to be an unforgettable ride! Let's dive into a world that your history books only hint at, a world filled with sails, swords, and smugglers...

Explanation of Piracy and Smuggling

Let's imagine you're on a large wooden ship in the middle of the ocean. Suddenly, another ship hoists a black flag with a skull and crossbones. Pirates! They rush onto your ship, brandishing swords and shouting loudly. They take everything they can grab - barrels of food, chests of gold, even the captain's fancy hat. That, my friends, is piracy.

Pirates were the outlaws of the sea, living by their own rules and taking what they wanted. They usually operated in crews, led by a captain. And while pirates often had a reputation for being ruthless and scary, not all of them were. Some pirates were seen as heroes by the common people, because they often shared their stolen wealth with those less fortunate. But whether they were seen as villains or heroes, there's no doubt that pirates led thrilling lives filled with danger and adventure.

Now, smuggling might sound less thrilling than piracy, but don't be fooled. Imagine you're sneaking through the dark, carrying a bag full of precious spices. You have to be silent, swift, and smart to avoid the guards who would take away your goods and throw you in jail. That's the life of a smuggler.

Smugglers were people who transported goods illegally. This usually meant without paying taxes or duties. They took advantage of the dark of night, secret routes, and clever hiding places to move their goods. Smugglers played a crucial role in colonial times, bringing in goods that were in high demand but heavily taxed or banned by the authorities.

Time frame (1650-1780)

Our swashbuckling journey takes place between the years 1650 and 1780. This period includes what is often known as the "Golden Age of Piracy," as well as the Revolutionary War. It's when some of the most famous (or infamous) pirates sailed the seas, and smuggling was at its peak. During these years, the world was changing rapidly. New lands were being explored, colonies were growing, and trade was increasing. But with this growth came conflict and opportunity - perfect conditions for piracy and smuggling to thrive.

Introduction to the main geographical areas: Europe, the Caribbean, Africa, and the original 13 colonies of the USA

In our adventure, we'll explore four main areas: Europe, the Caribbean, Africa, and the original 13 colonies of the United States.

In Europe, powerful nations like England, Spain, and France were busy establishing colonies and trade routes across the world. Ships were constantly sailing from their ports, loaded with goods for trade or settlers looking for a new life. But these ships were often targets for pirates, who saw them as floating treasure chests.

The Caribbean, with its many islands and hidden coves, was the perfect playground for pirates and smugglers. It was here that many pirates had their bases, hiding their stolen treasures and planning their next attack. Smugglers also loved the Caribbean, using the islands as stops along their secret routes.

Africa played a vital yet heartbreaking role in this story. As part of the triangular trade route between Europe, Africa, and the American colonies, Africa became a significant player. This was a time when many Africans were captured and sold as slaves, often by pirates and smugglers.

And then there were the 13 colonies in America. These new settlements were often the end destination for the goods smuggled from Europe and the Caribbean. Pirates also targeted the colonies, attacking their ports and ships. The colonies played a crucial role in our story, as they were deeply affected by both piracy and smuggling during this period.

If you enjoy this book, please leave a 5-star review on Amazon because it will help other students find it. Also, follow me on Amazon to see other books you might like.

Chapter One: A Pirate's Life

Definition of a Pirate

Pirates, who were they? In a nutshell, pirates were the rule-breakers of the sea. They didn't obey the laws of any nation or king. Instead, they lived by their own rules, sailing the high seas and taking whatever they wanted.

But did you know that not all pirates started out as lawbreakers? Some were privateers, sailors who were given permission by their government to attack enemy ships during war. However, when the war ended, many found they preferred the freedom and riches of their previous life and turned to piracy.

Life on a Pirate Ship

Life on a pirate ship was nothing like what you might see in movies. It was a hard and often short life. Pirates were constantly on the move, looking for ships to rob. They had to face dangerous sea battles, violent storms, and the threat of being caught and hanged.

Pirates ate whatever they could get their hands on, often surviving on hardtack, a type of dry biscuit, and whatever meat or fish they could catch. And while it might sound exciting to be on a ship full of treasure, the truth is, many pirates often ended up spending their loot as quickly as they got it.

But it wasn't all hardship. Pirates also knew how to have fun. They would sing songs, known as sea shanties, to keep their spirits up and to help pass the time during long voyages. They also loved to tell tall tales and play games.

The Pirate Code of Conduct

Believe it or not, pirates had their own set of rules known as the Pirate Code. This was a set of agreements that all crew members had to follow. It included things like how the loot would be divided, what would happen if a pirate got injured, and punishments for breaking the rules.

One famous Pirate Code was that of the legendary pirate Bartholomew Roberts, also known as Black Bart. His code included rules such as "no man shall gamble for money" and "lights and candles should be put out at eight o'clock at night". If a pirate broke these rules, they could be marooned on a deserted island or even thrown overboard!

Aboard the Pirate Ship

Pirate ships varied in size and design, but most were chosen for speed and maneuverability. They needed to be fast enough to chase down other ships and sturdy enough to withstand the rough seas and cannon fire.

On the ship, each pirate had a role. The captain was in charge, but unlike in navy ships, pirate captains were often chosen by the crew and could be voted out. Other roles included the quartermaster, who was second in command, the boatswain, responsible for the maintenance of the ship, the surgeon, who took care of the injured, and the cook. Yes, even pirates needed someone to cook their meals.

The center of the ship was usually where the cannons were kept, ready for battle. Below that was the hold, where they stored the loot, food, and other supplies. And right at the bottom was the bilge, the lowest part of the ship, which was often filled with seawater, rats, and other less than pleasant things. This was where disobedient pirates might be sent as a punishment.

Daily Life at Sea: Pirate Provisions and 'Nature's Calls'

Pirates are most often remembered for their daring high-seas adventures and treacherous exploits, but what about the less glamorous aspects of their day-to-day life at sea? The intricacies of pirate life such as eating habits and bodily necessities are not often the topics of grand tales, but they are essential for a full understanding of the pirates' historical reality.

On a pirate ship, the food wasn't exactly a gourmet meal. A pirate's diet primarily consisted of salted or smoked meats, hardtack (a type of hard, dry biscuit), dried beans, cheese, and occasionally some pickled or preserved fruits and vegetables. The lack of fresh food often led to health problems such as scurvy, a vitamin C deficiency that caused symptoms like anemia, edema, and severe fatigue. This deficiency was sometimes countered by consuming citrus fruits like lemons and limes when they were available.

Preparing meals on the ship was a communal task. Ships often had a 'ship's cook,' who was typically an older or injured pirate who could no longer participate in the physical exertion required during raids. The cook would prepare meals in a large pot over a fire, often making stews or soups to soften the hardtack and salted meat. This meal was typically served twice a day, at midday and in the evening.

Drinking water was often a scarce commodity, especially on long voyages. Stored in wooden casks, water would quickly become stale and develop algae, making it unpalatable. Pirates would often drink beer or rum as an alternative, leading to the stereotypical image of the hard-drinking pirate. Rum, in particular, was popular among pirates. The infamous "pirate's grog" was a mixture of rum, water, lemon juice, and a bit of sugar.

Addressing nature's call aboard a pirate ship was a bit more complicated than preparing a meal. The ship's design typically included a specific area known as 'the head,' located at the front (or the bow) of the ship. This was the designated place for pirates to relieve themselves. The reason for its location was practical: the bow of the ship was where the wind usually came from while sailing, meaning the smell wouldn't blow back across the ship.

These facilities were incredibly basic, often just consisting of a hole cut into a plank extended over the edge of the ship. Privacy was not a luxury afforded on pirate ships; pirates would have to go about their business in full view of the crew. For more serious matters, a bucket might be used, which would then be emptied overboard. In rough seas, these tasks could become particularly challenging.

Understanding these everyday realities of life aboard a pirate ship helps to humanize these often-mythologized figures. Despite their swashbuckling image, pirates had to grapple with the same basic needs as everyone else, often under challenging conditions. Their diet and sanitary conditions paint a picture of harsh realities, far removed from the romanticized depictions of pirate life.

The Mighty Vessels: Navigating the High Seas in the 17th and 18th Centuries

The story of piracy and adventure on the high seas during the 17th and 18th centuries wouldn't be complete without the ships that made these voyages possible. Pirates, smugglers, privateers, and the British Navy all utilized a variety of vessels, each with its unique specifications and capabilities. To a pirate or sailor of this era, their ship was their home, their fortress, and their means of exploration and survival.

Let's start with the **Sloop**. Sloops were small, fast vessels that were a favorite among pirates and smugglers. They were typically single-masted, meaning they had one large pole, or mast, where sails were attached. The sloop's sails were usually a combination of a large mainsail (the one in the center) and a smaller jib (a triangular sail at the front). With their shallow draft (how deep the bottom part of the ship, the hull, goes into the water), sloops could easily navigate the shallow waters of the Caribbean and North American coastlines where larger ships couldn't venture. These features made sloops ideal for quick getaways, surprise attacks, or stealthy smuggling operations. The crew of a sloop could range from a handful of men to around 75 on larger ones.

The **Brigantine** was another popular type of ship during this era, particularly among pirates. It was larger than a sloop, typically carrying 100 to 200 men. A brigantine had two masts, with square sails (shaped like a rectangle) on the foremast (the front one) and a gaff-rigged mainsail (a four-sided sail) on the mainmast (the back one). This mix of sails gave the brigantine both speed and maneuverability. Its larger size also meant it could carry more cannons, usually between 10 and 20, giving it a considerable punch in a naval battle.

Next, we have the **Frigate**. These were the warhorses of the British Navy but were also loved by privateers and pirates lucky enough to capture one. Frigates were large, three-masted ships with a focus on speed and firepower. They were usually armed with 20 to 50 cannons, placed in a continuous row along the sides of the ship, known as a gun deck. This arrangement allowed them to unleash a broadside attack, firing all cannons on one side at once for a devastating effect. Frigates often had separate quarters for officers and had larger, more comfortable living spaces compared to smaller vessels.

Another noteworthy ship was the **Galleon**. These grand vessels were mainly used by the Spanish for transporting treasure from the New World back to Spain. Galleons were large, heavily armed ships with three or four masts covered in square sails, allowing them to carry large amounts of cargo. They were slower and less maneuverable than other ship types, making them vulnerable to attacks by quicker pirate ships. The crew on a Galleon could range from 200 to 800 men, depending on the size of the ship.

Finally, there were the mighty **Ships-of-the-Line**, the largest and most powerful vessels in the British Navy. These ships, also known as line-of-battle ships, were designed for engaging the enemy in a line formation, where each ship would follow the one in front in a straight line, unleashing their cannons at the enemy. Ships-of-the-Line had three or four masts and two or more gun decks, carrying anywhere from 64 to over 100 cannons. The crew on a Ship-of-the-Line could be up to 850 men, including officers, sailors, marines, and often a chaplain and surgeon.

Crewing these ships was a demanding task. Sailors had to be skilled in many areas: navigating by stars, rigging sails, loading and firing cannons, repairing damage, and much more. The quarters were often cramped and uncomfortable, with many men sharing small spaces. The diet was basic, and fresh water was often in short supply on long voyages. Despite these hardships, life at sea offered many men a chance for adventure, and for some, a path to riches.

The term **"Man-of-War"** was often used to describe any powerful warship or frigate belonging to the Royal Navy of the colonial powers. Still, it is most commonly associated with a ship that could rightly be called the floating fortress of the seas.

The Man-of-War was an awe-inspiring sight. A large, imposing vessel, it was equipped with three masts and could carry up to 124 cannons spread over three gun decks. These guns weren't just any cannons. They were often a mix of different types, including the long-range, but less powerful, culverins and the short-range, but much more destructive, demi-cannons. This mixture of cannon types allowed the ship to engage enemies at various ranges effectively.

The size of a Man-of-War was its most intimidating feature. Depending on its size, a Man-of-War could carry anywhere from 250 to 850 sailors, soldiers, and officers. Each man had a role to play in the operation of the ship, whether it was handling sails, firing cannons, or keeping the vessel in working order. Man-of-War ships were more than just seafaring vehicles; they were floating military bases, complete with their own infirmaries and sometimes even a chapel.

Unlike other ships, Man-of-War ships were not built for speed or for smuggling. They were built for strength and firepower. They were often at the center of naval fleet formations, their powerful cannons providing a protective wall of firepower for smaller and more vulnerable ships in the fleet.

However, the strength of a Man-of-War was also its weakness. Its large size and heavy cannons made it slow and difficult to maneuver, particularly in close-range combat. This weakness made the Man-of-War an attractive target for small, fast pirate ships that could outmaneuver the large warship and attack it from the sides and rear.

In the hands of a skilled crew, however, a Man-of-War was a formidable adversary. Its sheer size and firepower made it a crucial tool for maintaining control of the seas during the 17th and 18th centuries. From the towering masts to the powerful cannons, the Man-of-War was a testament to naval engineering and a symbol of the might of the colonial powers.

So, whether it was the speedy sloop zipping through the shallow waters, the firepower-packed frigate, or the majestic Ship-of-the-Line, each of these vessels played a unique and vital role in shaping the era of piracy, smuggling, and naval warfare. These ships were not just tools of the trade, but homes to the men who lived, worked, and often died upon their decks. Their designs and capabilities helped shape the strategies, successes, and fates of those who sailed the high seas in the Age of Sail.

Fascinating Maritime Technology of the Time

When we think about technology, we often think of computers, smartphones, and other modern devices. However, technology in the 17th and 18th centuries, particularly aboard naval vessels like pirate ships, frigates, and Man-of-War, was just as vital and impressive for its time.

Navigational Instruments:
   Navigation was crucial for any vessel traversing the vast, unpredictable ocean. Basic tools like the compass were essential for determining the ship's course. However, other more complex devices were also employed.

The mariner's astrolabe was a valuable instrument that enabled seafarers to measure the altitude of the sun or a star above the horizon, which helped in determining latitude. Alongside the astrolabe, a quadrant or sextant was used, which could also measure the angle between two objects.

Navigational charts and maps, although primitive by today's standards, were crucial for planning voyages and avoiding known dangers. Dead reckoning, a process of calculating one's current position based on a previously known position and estimating speed and course over time, was also commonly used.

Ship's Construction:

Technological advances in shipbuilding during this period were significant. Better knowledge of dynamics and improvements in design made the ships faster, more maneuverable, and able to carry more cargo or armament.

Shipbuilders started to use more durable materials like oak and iron to reinforce the ship's structure. The hull's design was improved to allow better movement through water, and the masts and rigging were structured to maximize wind usage, improving the ship's speed and maneuverability.

Weaponry:

Cannons, the primary weaponry on any warship, were mounted on carriages that could be rolled in and out of gun ports. This technology allowed the crew to load and fire the cannons while minimizing their exposure to enemy fire.

Shot technology also improved, with different types of ammunition being used for various purposes. Chain shot, for example, was two cannonballs linked by a chain and was designed to destroy rigging and masts.

Communication:

Ships communicated with each other using a variety of signals. Flags of different colors and designs were used to relay messages from ship to ship. At night, lanterns were used in a similar way. The messages could be quite complex, with a sequence of flags or lights representing specific instructions or information.

Living Conditions:

Technologies used to improve the crew's living conditions were also crucial. Pumps were used to remove bilge water from the bottom of the ship, an area that could otherwise become a breeding ground for disease. Cooking was done on a stove in the galley, and food was stored in barrels to prevent spoilage during long voyages.

Despite the harsh and often dangerous conditions, these technologies of the time played a vital role in helping sailors, pirates, and naval officers navigate the high seas and engage in maritime warfare. Although these systems may seem rudimentary by today's standards, they were groundbreaking at the time and paved the way for the advanced nautical technologies we have today.

Fun Facts

- Pirates didn't make people walk the plank. That's a myth made popular by movies and books. They had other punishments like marooning or keelhauling (which was dragging a person underwater from one end of the ship to the other).
- Pirates often had pets on board their ships. Cats were popular because they kept the rat population down.
- Pirates didn't really bury their treasure. Most of the time, they spent their loot as soon as they reached port. The idea of buried treasure comes from a few isolated cases and lots of pirate legends.
- Not all pirates were men. There were several famous female pirates like Anne Bonny and Mary Read who were just as

fierce and feared as their male counterparts.

- While we often associate pirates with phrases like "Arr matey!" and "Shiver me timbers!" — there's actually no historical evidence to suggest pirates spoke this way. The "pirate accent" you often hear in movies is actually based on actor Robert Newton's performance as Long John Silver in the 1950 film "Treasure Island". Real pirates probably didn't talk like that.
- Pirate ships were democratic. The captain was elected by the crew and they could vote to replace him. The crew also voted on important decisions.
- Ever heard of Blackbeard? His real name was Edward Teach. To appear more fearsome in battle, he would weave hemp into his beard and light it on fire. Talk about hot-headed!

Living the pirate life was definitely not easy, and it certainly wasn't for everyone. But for those who chose it, it was a life full of adventure, danger, and the chance for freedom and fortune. Remember, though, it was a dishonest living. In the next chapter, we'll dive into another shadowy profession of this era: smuggling. Hold on to your hats, because our swashbuckling journey is just getting started...

Chapter 1 Quiz

1. Pirates lived by a strict set of rules known as the __________________.

2. On a pirate ship, the __________________ was democratically elected by the crew.

3. Blackbeard's real name was __________________.

4. The punishment for not following the pirate's code was
    _________________.

5. The _________________ was a vital instrument that enabled
    seafarers to measure the altitude of the sun or a star above
    the horizon, which helped in determining latitude.

6. In the process of _________________, one calculates their
    current position based on a previously known position
    and estimates speed and course over time.

7. Shipbuilders in the 17th and 18th century started using
    more durable materials like oak and _________________ to
    reinforce the ship's structure.

8. The _________________, the primary weaponry on a warship,
    were mounted on carriages that could be rolled in and out
    of gun ports.

9. _________________ shot, which was two cannonballs linked by
    a chain, was designed to destroy rigging and masts.

10. Ships communicated with each other using a variety of
    signals, including flags of different colors and designs
    during the day and _________________ at night.

11. The _________________ was used to remove bilge water from the
    bottom of the ship, an area that could otherwise become a
    breeding ground for disease.

12. A _________________ ship was a powerful, heavily armed ves-
    sel, used by the British Navy between the 16th and 19th
    centuries.

13. A _________________ was a fast, medium-sized ship, used
    primarily for warfare and piracy.

14. The _________________ was a small, fast ship, used by smug-
    glers and privateers to quickly navigate through waters.

Chapter Two: Smuggling – A Risky Game

Explanation of Smuggling

Smuggling. It sounds like a sneaky word, doesn't it? And rightly so. Smuggling was, and still is, all about sneaking things from one place to another without getting caught. It might sound simple, but it was a risky game that required wit, bravery, and a lot of secrecy.

In the days of pirates and colonial America, smuggling was a big business. Smugglers transported all kinds of goods, from spices to fabric, avoiding official trade routes and sneaking past custom officers. Why? To avoid paying taxes and to bring in items that were banned or limited. But being a smuggler wasn't an easy job. It required careful planning, a daring spirit, and the ability to stay calm under pressure.

Reasons Why People Became Smugglers

Just like piracy, people became smugglers for many different reasons. Some were drawn to the thrill and danger of it, while others were desperate and saw it as their only option. But for many, the biggest attraction was the potential for making a lot of money.

You see, in those days, governments put heavy taxes on many everyday items that people needed to make clothes, tools, and other things. They did this to control trade and to fill their coffers. But these taxes often made goods very expensive, and sometimes people couldn't get what they needed. This is where smugglers saw an opportunity. By avoiding taxes and sneaking goods into the colonies, smugglers could sell them for less while still making a profit.

During the colonial period, the British government implemented a series of laws and regulations known as the Navigation Acts to control trade between England and its colonies. These laws were designed to ensure that England benefited economically from its colonies by regulating what goods could be imported and exported, and where these goods could come from or go to.

One of the most notable goods that were restricted was molasses. The Molasses Act of 1733 placed high taxes on molasses imported from non-British colonies in an effort to control the rum industry. However, this led to widespread smuggling as colonial merchants sought cheaper sources of molasses for their rum distilleries.

In addition to molasses, the Navigation Acts also heavily regulated the import of textiles, particularly woolen goods. The British Wool Act of 1699 was designed to protect England's wool industry by prohibiting the export of wool from any of the colonies. Colonists were also prohibited from manufacturing their own woolen goods, which led to widespread dissatisfaction and smuggling of wool and woolen products.

Furthermore, the Hat Act of 1732 and the Iron Act of 1750 were imposed to restrict the manufacture of hats and iron goods in the colonies. These laws aimed to ensure that raw materials from the colonies were sent to Britain to be made into finished goods, which could then be sold back to the colonists at a profit.

So, while not all goods were outright banned, many were heavily taxed or their manufacture was restricted in the colonies, creating a system where British merchants benefitted at the expense of colonial merchants. This, in turn, led to a rise in smuggling and was one of the contributing factors to the growing dissatisfaction that eventually led to the American Revolution.

Goods That Were Smuggled During the Colonial Times

Smugglers moved a wide variety of goods, often items that were in high demand. Here are a few examples:

1. Tea: You've probably heard of the Boston Tea Party, where colonists protested against high tea taxes by dumping tea into the harbor. Well, tea was one of the most smuggled items.

Smugglers would bring in tea from places like the Netherlands, where it was cheaper, and sell it to the colonists who couldn't afford or didn't want to pay the high taxes on British tea.

2. Tobacco: Another highly taxed item was tobacco. As its popularity grew, so did the demand for cheap tobacco. Enter the smugglers, who brought in tobacco from all over the world, avoiding the heavy British taxes.

3. Textiles: Beautiful fabrics from India and China, like silk and calico, were banned by the British government to protect their own industries. But these fabrics were popular for their quality and designs. So, smugglers would sneak these banned textiles into the colonies.

4. Sugar and Molasses: These were key ingredients in making rum. The British tried to control the rum industry by putting high taxes on sugar and molasses from non-British islands. But smugglers found a way around this by bringing in these goods from French and Dutch islands.

5. Spices: Spices like ginger, cinnamon, cloves, and nutmeg (which are cheap and common nowadays) were highly valued and expensive in colonial times due to a combination of factors including their rarity, demand, and the complexity of their trade routes. Here's why...

Rarity and Difficulty in Cultivation: Many spices came from specific regions and were difficult to cultivate elsewhere. For example, cloves and nutmeg were only grown in the Moluccas, also known as the Spice Islands, in what is now Indonesia. The difficulty in growing these spices made them rare commodities.

Long and Dangerous Trade Routes: Spices had to travel long distances from places like the East Indies, India, and Southeast Asia to reach Europe and colonial America. These spice routes were dangerous, traversing rough seas and hostile territories. Pirates, storms, and even simple spoilage could ruin a shipment, making each successful delivery more valuable.

High Demand: Spices were in high demand for a variety of reasons. They were used for preserving and flavoring food, in medicines, and even for rituals or religious ceremonies. In a time without refrigeration, spices were crucial for making preserved foods palatable.

Monopolies and Taxes: The spice trade was tightly controlled by powerful entities such as the British and Dutch East India Companies. These companies held monopolies over the trade, which allowed them to set high prices. Additionally, taxes imposed by governments also added to the cost.

Symbol of Status: Possessing and using spices was seen as a sign of wealth and social status. The ability to afford and consume these exotic substances was a way for people to show off their wealth, which drove up demand and prices.

So, the value and cost of spices in the 1700s weren't just about the spices themselves. They were also a reflection of the difficulties and dangers of the spice trade, and the social prestige associated with these exotic goods.

The Secret Dealings of Colonial Smugglers

Consider the tale of Frederick Philipse, a prominent New York City merchant in the late 17th and early 18th centuries. Philipse was a member of the city's high society, but beneath his respectable facade, he was deeply involved in smuggling activities.

Philipse made his fortune through trade, but he wasn't satisfied with just being a lawful businessman. He was suspected of dealing in goods smuggled from the Dutch and French colonies in the Caribbean, which was illegal since the English Navigation Acts required all goods to pass through England before being sold in the colonies.

In the 1690s, Philipse built the Old Dutch Church of Sleepy Hollow, a beautiful stone church that's still standing today. But according to local legends, the church wasn't just a place of worship—it was also a hub for Philipse's smuggling operations.

Hidden compartments beneath the church floorboards were reportedly used to store smuggled goods, while the church's tall steeple served as a lookout point. When a ship carrying illicit goods approached, a lantern was hung from the steeple as a signal to the ship's crew that it was safe to come ashore.

But despite these cunning methods and his high status, Philipse couldn't keep his illicit activities a secret forever. His smuggling was eventually exposed, and in 1701, he was removed from his position on the New York Governor's Council. Nevertheless, he managed to avoid serious punishment and continued his smuggling operations until his death in 1702.

Philipse's story is a perfect example of how smuggling wasn't just the work of shady characters or pirates—it also involved respected members of society, who used their wealth and power to bend the rules for their own gain.

Fun Facts

- Did you know that even some of America's Founding Fathers were involved in smuggling? John Hancock, a prominent figure in the American Revolution, was accused of smuggling wine to avoid taxes.
- During colonial times, smuggling was considered by many as a form of protest against the unfair taxes imposed by the British government. It was a way for the colonists to fight back.
- Smugglers often used secret codes and signs to communicate with each other and to mark safe houses.

The world of smuggling was full of intrigue and risk. But for those who were brave enough to play the game, it could also be a world of great reward. As we continue our journey, we'll see how smuggling played a key role in shaping the history of colonial America. So, keep your wits about you, we've got more thrilling, true stories about pirates coming soon...

Chapter 2 Quiz:

1. Smuggling was often used as a means to evade _________________ imposed by colonial powers.
2. The most commonly smuggled goods were _________________ and _________________.
3. The smuggling method that involved hiding goods in secret compartments was called _________________.
4. Pirates and smugglers often used _________________ to communicate with each other.

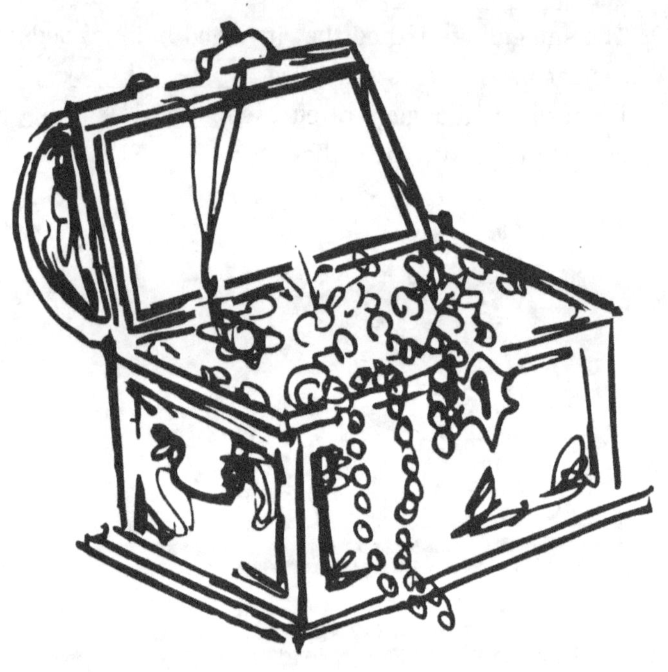

Chapter Three: Colonial America – A Pirate's Playground

Overview of the Original 13 Colonies

The 13 original colonies! Ah, what an adventurous time and place. These were the British colonies in North America, founded between 1607 and 1732. They were Delaware, Pennsylvania, New Jersey, Georgia, Connecticut, Massachusetts Bay, Maryland, South Carolina, New Hampshire, Virginia, New York, North Carolina, and Rhode Island and Providence Plantations. Quite a mouthful, isn't it?

These colonies were like little siblings, all unique, yet part of one family. Each had its personality, its way of doing things, and its dreams. Some, like Virginia, were founded for business reasons. Others, like Massachusetts Bay, were founded for religious freedom. The colonies were a mix of thriving towns and rural communities, from bustling ports filled with sailing ships to farmland where tobacco and cotton grew.

But life wasn't always easy in the colonies. The settlers had to contend with harsh winters, diseases, and often strained relations with the Native American tribes. Despite these challenges, they built homes, raised families, and established communities with schools and churches.

In the cities, you could find a blend of different cultures and backgrounds. You had people from England, of course, but also from Scotland, Ireland, Germany, and even African slaves. Despite the hardships, these colonies were alive with promise and potential.

Delaware: Delaware, initially known as New Sweden due to its early Swedish settlers, was an area with a tumultuous history. The Swedish, Dutch, and English all staked claims on it at different times. Its prime location on the Delaware River made it an attractive target for pirates seeking easy access to ships laden with goods. Local authorities often struggled to control these pirates due to the shifting governance of the region.

Pennsylvania: Known as "Penn's Woods," Pennsylvania was founded by William Penn as a haven for Quakers. Its bustling city of Philadelphia became a major trade center, attracting pirates eager for loot. However, Penn's effective governance and a well-regulated militia kept piracy relatively in check compared to some other colonies.

New Jersey: This colony, located between the Hudson and Delaware rivers, was a strategic location for both legal trade and illegal activities. Pirates found the long coastline convenient for their activities, with local merchants often willing to trade in pirated goods.

Georgia: Founded as a debtor's colony by James Oglethorpe, Georgia was the last of the original colonies to be established. Due to its southern location, it became a hotspot for pirates who prowled the waters between the Carolinas and the Spanish colonies in Florida, leading to ongoing battles between pirates, colonists, and Spanish forces.

Connecticut: Connecticut's long coastline along Long Island Sound made it vulnerable to pirate raids. Yet, the colony also became infamous for harboring the notorious pirate Captain Kidd, who was even welcomed by some of its more unscrupulous inhabitants.

Massachusetts Bay: Boston, the biggest city in this colony, was a bustling port that attracted pirates due to the wealth flowing in and out of its harbor. Despite this, Massachusetts Bay also made significant efforts to suppress piracy, including trying and hanging pirates in Boston.

Maryland: Maryland, founded as a haven for English Catholics, had a flourishing tobacco trade that enticed pirates. However, Maryland also had a rigorous judiciary that tried and punished pirates, making it a risky territory for them.

South Carolina: With its major port at Charleston, South Carolina was a prime target for pirates. Its history is intertwined with pirates like Blackbeard and Stede Bonnet, and the colony's ongoing struggles to suppress piracy.

New Hampshire: This small northern colony, centered around the trade-heavy Portsmouth, was not immune to pirate activities. Still, harsh weather and vigilant authorities made it less impacted than some of its southern neighbors.

Virginia: Jamestown, the first permanent English settlement in the New World, was in Virginia. This prosperous colony, with its profitable tobacco plantations, attracted many pirates. Still, strong leadership and robust legal institutions kept them at bay.

New York: The diverse, trade-centric colony of New York was a magnet for pirates, offering a bustling black market for their stolen goods. Yet, it also underwent a shift in its approach to piracy, from initially lenient to more hostile following the infamous trial of Captain Kidd in 1701.

North Carolina: Known for its Outer Banks, a haven for pirates, North Carolina has a rich history of piracy. The infamous Blackbeard even considered it his base, allegedly with the governor's collusion.

Rhode Island and Providence Plantations: As the first colony to declare independence from British rule, Rhode Island was known for its spirit of rebellion. It was also known for its ambiguous relationship with pirates, often providing them safe haven while also serving as a center for pirate trials. Notorious pirate Thomas Tew was even a respected figure in Rhode Island society.

Why These Colonies Were Attractive to Pirates and Smugglers

Now, imagine you're a pirate or a smuggler in the 1700s. Where would you go? The answer is, where business was booming, where law enforcement was lax, and where there were plenty of hiding spots for your ship and your loot. And guess what? The 13 colonies offered all this and more.

Firstly, the colonies had busy ports. Cities like Charleston, Boston, and Philadelphia were bustling with merchant ships coming and going, laden with goods from across the globe. For a pirate, this was like a buffet of opportunities! They could capture these ships and seize their cargoes, from precious silver and gold to valuable commodities like tobacco and sugar.

Smugglers, on the other hand, loved the high taxes and trade restrictions imposed by Britain on the colonies. Remember the Navigation Acts we talked about earlier? They made certain goods very expensive, as they had to pass through England first. But smugglers could get these goods directly, avoiding the taxes and selling them cheaper. This made smuggling a profitable business, despite its risks.

Moreover, the vast coastline offered plenty of hiding spots. There were numerous bays, inlets, and rivers where pirates could anchor their ships unseen, or smugglers could land their illegal cargoes under cover of darkness. Places like the Outer Banks in North Carolina, with their shallow waters and treacherous shoals, were perfect for these purposes.

But perhaps what made the colonies most attractive to pirates and smugglers was the often blurry line between legal and illegal. In these growing communities, many people were willing to look the other way or even collaborate with pirates and smugglers. For instance, it's said that Blackbeard, one of the most notorious pirates, had an arrangement with Charles Eden, the Governor of North Carolina, providing him with protection in return for a share of his loot.

Triangular Trade: A Cycle that Touched Three Continents

In the 17th and 18th centuries, an era when ships were the most important mode of transportation connecting different parts of the world, the oceans were bustling with trade ships carrying all sorts of goods, making their way across the waves. The Triangular Trade was a system of trade that played a crucial part during this time, and involved three different regions: Europe, Africa, and the Americas.

What Was the Triangular Trade?

Imagine a big triangle drawn on a map of the Atlantic Ocean. At each point of the triangle is a region - Europe, Africa, and the Americas (specifically the 13 colonies and the Caribbean). This is where the Triangular Trade gets its name from.

The Triangular Trade was like a relay race but with ships. Ships from Europe would first stop in Africa, where they traded goods like guns, iron, and cloth for enslaved people. These people were captured in their homelands and forced onto the ships, beginning the brutal 'middle passage' across the Atlantic to the Americas. This was the second leg of the triangle. Once in the Americas, these enslaved people were traded for goods like sugar, tobacco, and cotton, which were very valuable in Europe. These goods were then loaded onto the ships for the final leg of the triangle, a return voyage to Europe.

Impact on the 13 Colonies and the Caribbean

The 13 American colonies and the Caribbean colonies played a critical role in the Triangular Trade. They were the source of many valuable resources. In the Caribbean colonies, the hot climate and fertile soil were perfect for growing sugar cane. In the Southern colonies, tobacco and cotton were the main crops. The plantations producing these goods relied heavily on the labor of enslaved people brought over from Africa.

In the northern colonies, less suitable for farming, people produced goods like rum, iron tools, and ship parts. Some of these products were shipped to Africa as part of the trade network. The 13 American colonies, from North to South, were a vital part of trans-Atlantic trade during the Golden Age of Piracy.

The African Tragedy

In Africa, the Triangular Trade had devastating effects. Millions of people were forcibly taken from their homes and families, packed into the cramped and inhumane conditions on ships, and transported across the Atlantic Ocean. Many did not survive the journey. Those who did survive were sold into a life of hard labor and brutal treatment in the Americas. This horrific trade in human lives left a scar on Africa that can still be felt today.

Pirates, Smugglers, and Privateers on the High Seas

The sea routes of the Triangular Trade were bustling with ships loaded with valuable goods, making them attractive targets for pirates, smugglers, and privateers. Pirates were outlaws who roamed the seas, attacking ships and stealing their cargo. Smugglers were traders who tried to avoid paying taxes on goods by secretly bringing them into port. Privateers were like legal pirates – individuals who were given permission by their government to attack and plunder enemy ships during war.

These groups added another level of danger and complexity to the Triangular Trade. Pirates could disrupt the trade, causing losses for the traders and changing the balance of goods. Smugglers could evade the system altogether, selling goods directly and avoiding taxes. Privateers, though they were sanctioned by governments, could still cause havoc and unpredictability in the system.

Understanding Our History

Studying the Triangular Trade helps us understand the connections between different parts of the world, the movement of goods and people, and the impact of these connections on societies. It's a reminder of a dark time in history, but it's also a story of how economies and societies were shaped and how they evolved. Understanding history helps us understand the world we live in today. It can also inspire us to work towards a better future where such injustices are a thing of the past. The world is interconnected, and every action has an impact. Learning about the past can help us make better decisions for the future.

Fun Facts

- Do you know that pirates didn't just steal treasure? They often took practical items like food, ropes, and sails, or even the ship itself. They could use these for their voyages or sell them for a pretty penny.
- Many pirates found support among the colonies' locals who were frustrated with British rule and high taxes. This made it easier for pirates to blend into society, sell their stolen goods, and even recruit crew members.
- Pirates often used the colonies as a place to rest and repair their ships after long voyages at sea. The natural harbors and abundance of resources made the American coastline an ideal pit-stop.
- Not only did the colonists sometimes collaborate with the pirates, but some pirates also ended up becoming

privateers! Privateers were essentially "legal pirates" who were given permission by a government (in this case, the British) to attack and loot enemy ships, especially during times of war. This fine line between pirate and privateer made the colonies an even more attractive and complex environment for seafaring outlaws.

Chapter 3 Quiz:

1. The pirate-friendly colony where Blackbeard once made his base was ______________.
2. Many of the original 13 colonies had ______________ which made them attractive to pirates and smugglers.
3. ______________ was a haven for Quakers.
4. ______________ was the most trade-centric colony.
5. Triangular Trade gets its name from the three-point route that connected ______, ______, and ______.
6. The ships loaded with goods from Europe sailed to ______ where these goods were traded for enslaved people.
7. In the ______ colonies, tobacco and cotton were the main crops.
8. The bustling trade routes of the Triangular Trade attracted the attention of ______, ______, and ______.

Chapter Four: Famous Pirates & Their Activities in the Colonies

The Golden Age of Piracy is typically considered to have spanned the years from around 1650 to around 1730. This era is often divided into three distinct periods: the buccaneering period (about 1650 to 1680), the pirate round (from around 1690 to 1700), and the post-Spanish Succession period (1715 to 1730).

The start of the Golden Age is marked by an increase in maritime trade and exploration, while the end is usually associated with increased efforts by colonial authorities and naval powers to suppress piracy. However, it should be noted that these dates are approximations invented by historians much later. Piracy, privateering, and smuggling existed both before and after this era and affected colonial America and the Revolutionary War (as you'll learn later).

Several larger than life characters were infamous during this time. Let's take a look at a few of them...

Escape and Evasion: The Audacious Adventures of Captain Thomas Pound

During the thrilling era of the 17th and 18th centuries, a veritable shadow economy arose on the bracing shores of Massachusetts. Piracy thrived, and one of the most noteworthy episodes during this period centers around a notorious pirate, Captain Thomas Pound, who had an extraordinary encounter with the colonial authorities in Boston. His bold actions, despite his ultimately unsuccessful endeavor, would leave an indelible mark on the region's pirate lore.

The year was 1689, and the colonial settlement of Massachusetts, already no stranger to the exploits of pirates, was about to experience a spectacle the likes of which it had seldom seen before. Captain Thomas Pound, an experienced British Navy sailor, was on the run. Having decided to abandon his life of official seafaring for the allure of piracy, Pound had become a thorn in the side of colonial authorities, and a hero among those who were less law-abiding.

In the wake of a string of audacious raids along the New England coast, Pound was caught in the act by British authorities and imprisoned in Boston. However, this tenacious pirate was not one to stay confined for long. With a band of fellow pirates and sympathizers, he managed to get out of jail.

Once out, Pound and his companions didn't waste time laying low. They quickly seized a vessel, the sloop "William and Mary," and set sail, intending to wreak havoc on the sea lanes once more. Massachusetts Bay was soon buzzing with news of the daring escape, and a frantic search began. The authorities vowed to bring Pound and his crew to justice.

Soon, the runaway pirates found themselves pursued by the British naval sloop "HMS Rose," captained by the steely-eyed and indefatigable Samuel Pease. After several days of cat-and-mouse maneuvering, a tense and fiery battle ensued. Pound, despite the odds stacked against him, fought valiantly, but the well-trained crew of the "HMS Rose" eventually overpowered the pirates. In heavy fighting Pound suffered gunshot wounds and Mary's captain, Samuel Pease, was killed. They were captured and returned to Boston amidst much public excitement.

Pound was subsequently tried and found guilty of piracy. Pound was put on a ship and taken to England to serve out his sentence. The ship was out to sea when a French privateer attacked it. Pound heroically battled for his British captors, but his partner, Hawkins, was slain during the fighting against the French privateers. Upon arriving in England, Pound had his sentence commuted, and after serving a brief period in jail, he was freed.

Pound's brief stint as a pirate was apparently forgotten once his naval status was restored and he was subsequently granted command of his own ship. He died in 1703. Based on his experiences, he developed a map of New England that featured the first useful chart of Boston Harbor. For the following 70 years, seafarers would consult the "Pound Chart" as their de facto map of Boston's waterfront.

Captain Thomas Pound's audacious escapade was widely reported and has since been passed down in Massachusetts folk-lore. This remarkable episode exemplifies the often-blurred lines between pirates and the colonial society they inhabited. The colonial period in Massachusetts was fraught with such thrilling episodes, encapsulating the audacious, complex, and often daringly rebellious spirit of piracy in Colonial America.

Captain Thomas Tew — Rhode Island's Pirate Hero

Rhode Island, a picturesque gem of New England, played host to a curious chronicle in the annals of pirate history during the late 17th century. It involved a man named Thomas Tew, who would later be known as the Rhode Island Pirate. His story, remarkable and filled with twists and turns, perfectly encapsulates the mingling of lawlessness, ambition, and eventual redemption that epitomized the pirate era.

In the early 1690s, Newport, Rhode Island, was a thriving center of colonial American life, bustling with trade and teeming with diversity. It was here that Thomas Tew, an unassuming and seemingly average mariner, decided to embrace the life of a pirate. He procured the support of fellow Rhode Islanders for his adventurous ambition to commandeer a ship to the Indian Ocean. There, he aimed to raid the rich vessels of the Moghul Empire, a risky plan that required cunning, courage, and a touch of madness.

Tew's maiden voyage as a pirate captain was phenomenally

successful. Aboard his ship, the "Amity," he captured an Arabian ship off the coast of Madagascar laden with jewels and precious metals. The bounty was beyond what any of them had dared to dream. In this single exploit, Tew had etched his name in pirate lore and became a legendary figure amongst his peers. His one-shot method of making a massive score, rather than many smaller raids, earned him the nickname of the "Rhode Island Pirate."

Upon returning to Newport, Tew was hailed as a hero by the local population. His incredible fortune, however, attracted the attention of the colonial authorities. It is said that instead of punishing Tew, the then-governor of Rhode Island, Walter Clarke, was swayed by the promise of increased wealth. Clarke, along with other influential individuals, invested in Tew's future endeavors along the "Pirate Round," effectively giving legitimacy to his piratical activities. This surprising turn of events, where authorities turned a blind eye to piracy for their gain, was not uncommon during the era.

Tew's second expedition, however, met with disaster. In a fierce battle with a ship near the Straits of Bab-el-Mandeb, Tew was fatally wounded, bringing an abrupt end to his brief yet impactful pirate career.

Tew's tale is fascinating, not just for his audacious acts of piracy but also for the complicit involvement of the colonial authorities. It sheds light on how piracy was often interwoven with politics and economics during the colonial era, which you'll learn more about later in this book. The Rhode Island Pirate's tale is a captivating blend of high-seas adventure, colonial power play, and an individual's audacity, painting a rich tableau of piracy in Rhode Island during the 17th century.

The Unlikely Pirate: Stede Bonnet's High Sea Adventures

While the seas of the Golden Age of Piracy were filled with fearsome marauders and grizzled seadogs, few pirates were as unlikely as Stede Bonnet. Born into a wealthy English family, Bonnet seemed to be destined for a life of privilege and comfort. But, in 1717, he turned his back on his genteel existence to become one of the most notorious pirates in the Caribbean – earning him the nickname, the "Gentleman Pirate."

Stede Bonnet was born into a life of comfort and privilege in the British colony of Barbados. After inheriting his father's substantial sugar plantation, Bonnet seemed to have everything a man could want. But behind the facade of affluence and prestige, Bonnet was a deeply troubled man. His wife's constant nagging drove him to the brink of despair. And so, in the midst of a mid-life crisis, Bonnet decided to abandon his life of privilege for a life of adventure and peril on the high seas.

Unlike most pirates who rose from the seafaring ranks, Bonnet had no sailing experience. He purchased a sloop, named it the Revenge, and hired a crew to man it. His decision to enter piracy bewildered his friends and family, and the novelty of a "gentleman" turning pirate made him a topic of conversation throughout the colonies, from the sugar plantations of

Barbados to the coastal towns of Georgia.

Bonnet's foray into piracy started with the plunder of vessels off the coast of Virginia and the Carolinas. While his lack of seafaring experience made him an inept captain, the size of his vessel and his ruthlessness in battle made him a threat. Bonnet and his crew targeted mostly English vessels, seizing their goods and burning their ships. Despite his inexperience and unusual entry into piracy, Bonnet's exploits would cement his reputation as one of the most notorious pirates of his time.

Bonnet set off in September 1717 for Nassau, a notorious pirate haven on the island of New Providence in the Bahamas. He came upon a Spanish man-of-war, engaged it in combat, and managed to flee. His ship, "Revenge," sustained significant damage as a result of the fight. Bonnet was badly wounded and half of the ship's crew were killed or injured. When Bonnet arrived at Nassau, he replaced his wounded and re-equipped the Revenge with twelve cannons. At Nassau, Bonnet first encountered Captain Benjamin Hornigold and Edward Teach, aka Blackbeard, who had a significant impact on the rest of Bonnet's life. Due to his injuries, which rendered him unable to command the Revenge, Bonnet temporarily handed over control to Blackbeard while continuing to sail as a guest of the more seasoned pirate commander. Blackbeard and Bonnet pillaged eleven ships in Delaware Bay.

Blackbeard later double crossed Bonnet and stole his ship. Bonnet got a pardon from the governor of North Carolina and wanted to go privateering against the Spanish. But, with a small crew and ship, and few supplies, he was forced back into piracy under a different name to finance his career as a privateer. Bonnet's career, however, would not last. In 1718, he was captured near the mouth of the Cape Fear River by Colonel William Rhett of South Carolina. He was tried and executed for piracy in Charleston, marking an ignominious end to his tumultuous career.

Stede Bonnet's brief but eventful career as a pirate left a lasting impression on the early history of the southern colonies. He was the quintessential gentleman pirate, proof that anyone, regardless of their background, could be lured into the world of piracy by the promise of freedom and adventure. His audacious exploits and unusual origin story made him a legend, and his tale still echoes through the annals of piracy, a reminder of a time when the seas were a realm of danger, opportunity, and unbounded freedom.

Blackbeard's Reign: The Pirate King of North Carolina's Coastal Shadows

Blackbeard, the infamous pirate who stalked the seven seas, had a favorite haunt that he was especially fond of - North Carolina. There's no denying the allure this beautiful land held for him; from its endless stretches of sandy shores to the protective embrace of its numerous inlets and bays. But it was the Outer Banks, a 200-mile string of narrow barrier islands, where Blackbeard's tale turned from fascinating to legendary.

The tale begins in 1716 when a ferocious figure appeared on North Carolina's horizon. Edward Teach, better known as Blackbeard, had arrived. His long, fearsome beard and the slow-burning fuses he wore in his hat made for a terrifying sight. It was said that Blackbeard looked like a demon straight out of a sailor's worst nightmare.

Blackbeard's ship, the Queen Anne's Revenge, was as formidable as the man himself. A stolen French slave ship, it was retrofitted with 40 guns and enough space for a crew of 300. With this menacing vessel, Blackbeard terrorized the American coast and Caribbean Sea, waylaying ships and looting their treasures.

One of Blackbeard's most notorious escapades occurred in May 1718, when he blockaded the port of Charleston, South Carolina. For about a week, he plundered nine ships attempting to enter or leave the harbor, seizing goods and holding several prominent citizens hostage. But it wasn't gold or jewels that he demanded for their safe return - it was a chest of medicine. Once his unusual ransom was paid, Blackbeard released the hostages and sailed north, towards North Carolina.

Why was North Carolina so attractive to Blackbeard? Well, the shallow waters and treacherous sandbars of the Outer Banks provided natural protection against larger naval vessels. But the key to his audacious exploits was a certain Charles Eden, the Governor of North Carolina. Rumors suggested that Eden turned a blind eye to Blackbeard's activities in exchange for a share of his spoils. Whether it was a dishonest alliance or merely a lack of resources to combat the formidable pirate, Blackbeard was essentially given free rein over the region.

His base was in the coastal town of Bath, North Carolina's first town, where he was said to have owned a home. Blackbeard's presence in Bath was an open secret. The residents, perhaps out of fear or maybe the benefits his illicit activities brought, welcomed him. He was even said to have married a local girl in a ceremony attended by Governor Eden himself.

Blackbeard ruled his watery kingdom with audacity and flair. Tales of his antics abound. There was the time when, in a fit of boredom, he allegedly lit slow-burning fuses under his hat, shrouding his head in thick, menacing smoke during a meal with his crew. This terrifying spectacle made him look even more like the devil himself, reinforcing his fearsome image.

Another favorite anecdote involved Blackbeard and a fellow pirate, Israel Hands. After a night of drinking, Blackbeard allegedly shot Hands in the knee without any warning. When asked why he'd done it, Blackbeard responded that if he didn't shoot one of his crew members now and then, they'd forget who he was!

But all pirate stories must come to an end, and Blackbeard's was no exception. In November 1718, Lieutenant Robert Maynard of the Royal Navy caught up with him at Ocracoke Island. A fierce battle ensued, where Blackbeard fought with the ferocity of a wild animal, despite suffering severe wounds. When his body was finally recovered, it was said to have five gunshot wounds and twenty slashes from swords.

Blackbeard's death signaled the end of an era. His body and severed head hung from Maynard's ship as a gruesome trophy, a stark reminder of the fate that befell pirates. But, despite his demise, Blackbeard's legend only grew. Tales of his buried treasures hidden around North Carolina spread like wildfire, driving many treasure hunters on fruitless quests.

One such story that still fascinates treasure seekers is the tale of Blackbeard's silver-plated skull. It is said that after his death, his skull was silver-plated and used as a drinking goblet in local taverns! This ghoulish relic, known as "Blackbeard's Cup," is still rumored to be in possession of some secretive collector.

However, Blackbeard's legacy in North Carolina goes beyond fanciful stories and fruitless treasure hunts. His life and death played a significant role in shaping the state's history. Following his death, North Carolina's Governor Eden was accused of piracy himself. The accusations eventually led to increased British oversight of the colonies, transforming the political landscape of North Carolina and its sister colonies.

Blackbeard's death also marked a turning point in the so-called "Golden Age of Piracy." His highly publicized demise served as a warning to pirates everywhere, and a concerted effort from naval forces around the world led to a significant decrease in piracy.

In many ways, the waters of North Carolina have never truly forgotten Blackbeard. His audacious exploits and daring escapades are a part of the state's rich history. Tourists flock to Bath and Ocracoke, hoping to catch a glimpse of the ghost of Blackbeard, his fierce, flaming silhouette forever sailing in their imaginations.

Blackbeard's larger-than-life persona, his fearsome reputation, and the fascinating tales that surround him have cemented his status as the world's most notorious pirate. From his audacious blockades to his dramatic death, every moment of his life was an adventure. Today, Blackbeard's name is not whispered in fear but said with a kind of awe and fascination. He is not just a character in a storybook but a significant part of North Carolina's past, an indelible figure who shaped the course of history, one pirate raid at a time.

Even in death, Blackbeard is still the undisputed king of pirates, his legend outlasting his life, making North Carolina forever his kingdom, a place where his spirit still haunts the windswept beaches, whispering tales of adventure to those who dare to listen.

Fun Facts

- Did you know that New Hampshire was named by Captain John Mason after his home county in southern England? He hoped the colony would prosper just like its namesake, famous for its successful fishing villages.
- Georgia was the only one of the 13 colonies to be governed directly by the British government. It was originally founded as a buffer against Spanish Florida. It wasn't until 1752, when the governance of the colony was handed over

to the King, that it became a royal colony.

- The tiny colony of Rhode Island was unique for its time in offering religious freedom to all its inhabitants. It became a safe haven for many people who faced religious persecution in other colonies, including Jews, Quakers, and Baptists.
- Pennsylvania, founded by William Penn, was designed to be a "holy experiment" with an ideal society based on democratic principles and religious tolerance. It was also one of the few colonies that didn't have an official church.

Chapter 4 Quiz:

1. During which centuries did the shadow economy of piracy thrive on the shores of Massachusetts?
2. What was the name of the notorious pirate who had an extraordinary encounter with the colonial authorities in Boston?
3. ___________ was a nobleman who got bored and became a pirate.
4. The Golden Age of Piracy was from _______________ to _______________.

Chapter Five: Europe – The Heart of Trade and Conflict

Importance of Europe in Colonial Trade

During the colonial period, Europe was the beating heart of global trade. Countries like England, France, Spain, Portugal, and the Netherlands were all vying for dominance on the high seas. They built massive fleets of ships to transport goods to and from their colonies in the Americas, Africa, and Asia.

Many of the goods that we use today, such as coffee, tea, sugar, and tobacco, were first brought to Europe during this period. These items were so prized that they became known as "luxury goods." They were expensive, but people were willing to pay high prices for them.

The European countries were in constant competition with each other for control of these trade routes. This competition often led to wars, which in turn led to more opportunities for pirates and smugglers.

The countries would often use their colonies as a way to get an edge in this competition. For instance, England's colonies in North America produced tobacco, a popular luxury good. To ensure they had a monopoly on this product, the English passed laws that said American tobacco could only be sold in England. This meant that the English could control the price of tobacco and ensure a steady supply for their citizens.

These laws were great for the European countries, but they weren't so great for the colonists. They were forced to sell their goods at low prices and buy expensive European goods. This led to a lot of frustration and anger, which would eventually explode in the form of the American Revolution. But that's a story for another time.

Fun Facts

- Did you know that coffee became popular in England after tea was heavily taxed, leading to the Boston Tea Party in the American colonies? The British sure loved their hot drinks!
- The "sugar triangle" was a famous trade route during this time. Ships would take iron and manufactured goods from Europe to Africa, then they would carry slaves from Africa to the Americas, and finally, they would bring sugar, tobacco, and other goods back to Europe.
- The Netherlands was known as the "warehouse of the world" because it was a major hub for goods coming from all over the world. They would store these goods in their warehouses and then sell them to other countries.

European Powers and Their New World Realms

England

From 1650 to 1780, England was emerging as one of the most dominant powers in the world. During this period, England went through the civil war, the Glorious Revolution, the formation of the United Kingdom, and the start of the Industrial Revolution. England's colonies in the New World were primarily along the eastern coast of North America, which would later become the original 13 states of the U.S. It also held numerous Caribbean colonies such as Jamaica and Barbados, known for their sugar plantations.

England was often in conflict with other European powers, especially Spain and France, over control of trade routes and colonies. English privateers were a significant part of these conflicts, often licensed to harass and loot Spanish and French vessels. England also had strict navigation acts, which led to rampant smuggling in the American colonies.

France

France, under the Bourbon monarchy, was one of the most influential European powers during this period. New France, as it was called, extended from present-day Quebec in Canada down to Louisiana in the U.S. The French colonies were primarily involved in the fur trade, with a focus on building alliances with Native American tribes rather than large-scale settlement.

France had ongoing rivalries with England and Spain, leading to various wars throughout the period. French privateers were active in these conflicts, while smuggling became prevalent due to the high demand for English goods in French colonies and vice versa.

Spain

The Spanish Empire was a formidable power, despite beginning to decline in the 17th century. It had extensive colonies in the Americas, including large parts of North and South America, the Caribbean, and the Philippines in Asia. The Spanish colonies were primarily involved in agriculture, mining, and ranching.

Spain had a longstanding conflict with England, often resulting in naval wars. The Spanish were renowned for their treasure fleets carrying gold and silver from the New World back to Spain. These treasure fleets were frequent targets for pirates and privateers, particularly English and Dutch ones.

Portugal

Portugal, a pioneer in exploration, had established a vast trading empire in the previous century, including Brazil in South America and various posts along the African coast. The mines and sugar plantations in Brazil were particularly lucrative.

Portugal often found itself at odds with Spain over territorial claims, resulting in the Treaty of Tordesillas, dividing the New World between them. Portuguese ships were targeted by pirates due to their lucrative cargo of sugar, spices, and precious stones.

The Netherlands

The Dutch Republic was a significant naval and economic power in this period. Its American colonies, known as New

Netherland, included parts of present-day New York, New Jersey, Delaware, and Connecticut. They also had colonies in several Caribbean islands. The Dutch West India Company controlled these colonies, focusing on trade rather than settlement.

The Netherlands was at constant odds with England over trade supremacy, resulting in several Anglo-Dutch wars. Dutch privateers, or "Sea Beggars," were notorious for their naval combat skills. The Dutch colonies, being less regulated than their English counterparts, were often hotspots for smugglers.

Role of European Powers in Piracy and Smuggling

The European powers didn't just play a passive role in the piracy and smuggling that occurred during the colonial period. In many cases, they actively encouraged it.

One of the ways they did this was by issuing "letters of marque." These were legal documents that allowed private citizens to attack and loot ships from enemy countries. The people who did this were known as "privateers." They were essentially legal pirates.

These privateers played a major role in the wars between the European powers. They disrupted enemy trade, captured valuable goods, and even fought in naval battles. Some of the most famous privateers included Sir Francis Drake of England and Jean Bart of France.

However, not all pirates started as privateers. Some were sailors who had turned to piracy after being left unemployed by the end of a war. Others were former slaves who had escaped from the plantations in the Caribbean.

While the European powers might have benefited from the actions of these pirates, they were also threatened by them. Pirates didn't always follow the rules, and they would often attack ships from their own country. To combat this, the European powers established naval patrols and offered rewards for the capture of famous pirates.

Yet despite these efforts, piracy and smuggling continued to thrive. The vast size of the oceans and the high demand for smuggled goods made it nearly impossible to eradicate these activities. Pirates and smugglers became an integral part of the global trade network, a shadowy undercurrent beneath the surface of legitimate commerce.

In particular, smuggling flourished as a response to the strict trade laws imposed by the European powers. As mentioned earlier, these laws often prevented the colonists from trading with anyone but their mother country. However, the colonists found these laws unfair, and they were eager to trade with other countries that could offer better prices. This is where smugglers came in.

Smugglers would secretly transport goods between the colonies and other countries, bypassing the official trade routes. They played a crucial role in keeping the colonial economies alive, especially during times of war when the official trade routes were often disrupted. They also provided the colonists with goods that were in short supply, such as firearms and ammunition, which were essential for their defense.

However, smuggling wasn't just about breaking the rules. It was a highly dangerous activity that required great skill and courage. Smugglers had to avoid naval patrols, navigate treacherous waters, and deal with the constant threat of piracy. They also had to have a thorough knowledge of the local geography in order to find hidden coves and secret passages where they could land their goods undetected.

Despite these challenges, many people were drawn to the life of a smuggler. It was a chance to make a fortune, a life of adventure and danger, a way to strike back against the unfair trade laws. It was a way of life that defined an era and shaped the course of history.

Fun Facts

- Privateers were considered so respectable that they were often treated like naval officers. They were allowed to carry a commission, which is a document that gives them the authority to perform certain tasks on behalf of the government.
- Smugglers used a variety of ingenious methods to hide their goods. For example, they might use false bottoms in their ships or hollow out the masts to create secret compartments.

Europe was indeed the heart of trade and conflict, its arteries pumping with the lifeblood of the colonial economy. It was a world of intrigue and adventure, a place where fortunes could be made and lost in the blink of an eye. It was a world that shaped the destiny of the American colonies, and its echoes can still be felt today.

Profiles of Renowned Privateers — Sir Francis Drake & Jean Bart

Sir Francis Drake: England's Sea Dragon

Let's time-travel back to the 16th century, the era of Queen Elizabeth I, known as the Elizabethan Age. England was a rising naval power, and amongst the briny sea dogs who propelled this maritime might, one name stood out - Sir Francis Drake, the daring sea captain who became a hero to the English but a pirate to the Spanish.

Francis Drake was born around 1540 in Tavistock, Devonshire. His early years were marked by hardship as his family fled religious persecution, finding refuge in a hulk of an old ship. Perhaps it was this early exposure to seafaring life that set young Francis on his path.

Drake began his nautical career on merchant and slave ships, but his life took a significant turn when he joined his cousin, Sir John Hawkins, on a privateering expedition. Privateering, you recall, was state-sanctioned piracy, a rather respectable way of terrorizing your nation's enemies.

In 1572, Drake embarked on his ambitious voyage to Central America, targeting Spanish treasure fleets. His most notable exploit during this expedition was the audacious raid on the heavily fortified Spanish city of Nombre de Dios, where he successfully plundered a significant amount of Spanish gold and silver.

His audacious raid on the Spanish Silver Train at Nombre de Dios in Panama in 1573 truly cemented Drake's place in history. It all began when Drake made an alliance with the Cimarrons, African slaves who had escaped from their Spanish masters. With their help, he learned about the Spanish Silver Train, a mule convoy that carried silver across the Isthmus of Panama from the Pacific side to the Caribbean port of Nombre de Dios.

Drake and his men ambushed the Silver Train in the dead of night. However, during the skirmish, Drake was injured, struck by an arrow in his leg. Despite his wound, he insisted on pressing on, encouraging his men by declaring, "I would have come even if I had to creep on my hands and knees."

When his men found the piles of silver bars, they were astounded. It was too much for them to carry away, and they were forced to bury some of it to retrieve later. So much treasure was left behind by Drake and his men at Nombre de Dios that it was said that for years after, one could find silver bars scattered in the jungle. Drake was so focused on the attack that he didn't notice his leg injury until his boot had filled with his blood. He'd been too busy ensuring his men filled their pockets with the silver!

This event marked Drake as the first Englishman to see the Pacific Ocean from the New World, but more importantly, it underlined his daring, strategic brilliance, and the tenacity that would make him a legend. Drake's success in raiding the Silver Train and his other exploits in the New World paved the way for English privateering and future colonization in the region

Drake's most famed voyage was his circumnavigation of the globe between 1577 and 1580 aboard the Golden Hind. Authorized by Queen Elizabeth I, the voyage was ostensibly for exploration and trade. Still, Drake couldn't resist the allure of Spanish treasure. He raided Spanish settlements along the South American coast and captured Spanish treasure ships, amassing vast wealth.

In 1588, Drake played a crucial role in defeating the Spanish Armada, a fleet assembled by Spain to invade England. Drake's strategic cunning and bold tactics, including the use of fire-ships, were instrumental in the English victory. Following this triumph, Drake was hailed as a national hero.

Sir Francis Drake's life was filled with daring adventures and audacious exploits. To the English, he was a hero, a champion of the crown, and a defender of the realm. To the Spanish, he was El Draque, the dragon, a fearsome pirate who left havoc in his wake.

Fun Facts

- Drake's ship, the Golden Hind, was originally named the Pelican. Drake renamed the ship in the middle of his journey around the world to honor his patron, Sir Christopher Hatton, whose crest was a golden 'hind,' a female deer.
- After his successful circumnavigation, Queen Elizabeth I personally knighted Drake aboard the Golden Hind.

Jean Bart: France's Fearless Sea Rover

Across the English Channel, another maritime legend was making waves, quite literally. Born in 1651 in Dunkirk, a town famous for its corsairs, Jean Bart was destined for the sea. Despite being unable to read or write, Bart rose from being a simple sailor to a celebrated admiral and a national hero of France.

Bart started his nautical career at a young age. By the age of 12, he was already at sea, serving on various fishing boats and merchant ships. When he was 20, he embarked on a different path as a privateer. The privateering commission gave him the right to attack enemy ships, and the young sailor took to his new role like a fish to water.

Jean Bart was a master of naval warfare, known for his bold tactics and fearless leadership. He was also known for his uncanny ability to escape from enemy hands. He was captured multiple times by the Dutch but managed to escape on each occasion, often under daring circumstances.

Bart's most famous exploit was the Battle of Texel in 1694 during the Nine Years' War. He captured a large Dutch convoy, ensuring that France did not starve during the harsh winter. His heroics at Texel earned him a promotion to admiral and won him the admiration and gratitude of a nation.

Jean Bart's life was one of adventure and daring exploits. His indomitable spirit, tactical brilliance, and sheer audacity made him a legend of the sea. His remarkable journey from humble beginnings to national hero is a testament to his exceptional skills and indomitable spirit. While Jean Bart is primarily known for his exploits in European waters, the New World was a vast stage for many privateers and pirates, and his activities affected shipments between Europe and the New World.

Fun Facts

- Bart was such a national hero that when he died in 1702, he was given a state funeral, and statues were erected in his honor.
- Bart's exploits were so famous that they were turned into songs and stories. He is still celebrated in Dunkirk every year during the 'Carnival of Dunkirk.'

Fiery Frontiers: The French and Indian War and the Underworld of Smuggling

The French and Indian War, fought in North America between Britain and France with their respective Indian allies, was part of a larger global conflict known as the Seven Years' War. This war was driven in large part by the rivalry between Britain, France, and Spain.

The French and Indian War, also known as the Seven Years' War, was a major conflict between Great Britain and France that took place from 1754 to 1763. This war had significant effects on piracy and smuggling, particularly in the American colonies. Here are some key points:

Increase in Privateering: At the onset of the war, both the French and British enlisted privateers, effectively legalizing piracy against each other's ships. Privateering became a popular and relatively risk-free way for people in the colonies to get involved in the war effort and make a profit.

Rise in Smuggling: As a result of the war, Great Britain found itself in heavy debt and began to increase taxation in its American colonies to fund the war effort. This led to a surge in smuggling as colonists tried to avoid the new taxes. Goods like molasses, rum, and other supplies were often smuggled to evade the new regulations and duties. This illicit trade was a significant factor leading to the American Revolution.

Closure of War-Induced Loopholes: During the war, many loopholes for legal and illegal trade opened up. With the end of the war and the signing of the Treaty of Paris in 1763, these loopholes closed as nations tried to regain control over trade. This led to a decline in overt piracy but an increase in smuggling as new regulations were imposed.

Piracy Turns Inland: With the tightening of control on seaborne trade, piracy moved inland. The Ohio and Mississippi rivers became hotspots for river piracy as the colonial frontier moved west.

Decline in Caribbean Piracy: With the end of the war, Britain's naval focus could return to the Caribbean, leading to a decline in piracy there.

Even Blackbeard began his seafaring career as a privateer during the War of the Spanish Succession, another major conflict between European powers. It's possible that without these large-scale conflicts and the privateering they encouraged, some of history's most famous pirates might never have taken up the profession.

Chapter 5 Quiz:

1. Sir Francis Drake was a famous _______________ from England.
2. Jean Bart was a renowned _______________ from France.
3. Sir Francis Drake was knighted after his successful _______________.
4. Jean Bart was famous for his victory in the Battle of _______________.

Chapter Six: The Caribbean – The Pirate's Paradise

Description of the Caribbean in Colonial Times

During colonial times, the Caribbean was a wonderland of islands, bright blue waters, golden beaches, and dense, un-explored jungles. Imagine a place where the sun always shines, the sea is full of colorful fish, and exotic birds fly across a clear blue sky. That was the Caribbean. But it was also a region teeming with danger, adventure, and hidden treasures.

It was not just the natural beauty that made the Caribbean unique; it was also its vibrant mix of cultures. From the indigenous Taino and Carib peoples to the European colonizers from Spain, France, England, and the Netherlands, to the African slaves brought to work on the sugar plantations, the Caribbean was a melting pot of different traditions, languages, and ways of life.

The islands of the Caribbean were prized possessions for the European powers. They were abundant in resources like sugar, tobacco, and indigo. Plantations popped up across the islands, creating a boom in the Atlantic trade. But it was the sugar plantations, with their need for constant labor, that fueled the transatlantic slave trade, a dark and tragic aspect of Caribbean history.

Who were the people living on the Caribbean islands when Europeans arrived and into the Golden Age of Piracy? Let's find out...

Fun Facts

- Sugar was sometimes called "white gold" because it was so valuable. It was the main reason why European powers fought so fiercely over the Caribbean islands.
- The Carib Indians were so fearsome and successful in defending their homes that the Caribbean Sea was named after them.

Paradise Found and Lost: The Forgotten Peoples of the Pirate's Paradise

The Taino: The Good People of the Caribbean

When Christopher Columbus first landed in the Americas in 1492, the first people he encountered were the Taino. They lived in what is now the Bahamas, Dominican Republic, Cuba, Greater Antilles, and the northern Lesser Antilles. The word

"Taino" means "good" or "noble" in their language, and they were indeed friendly and peaceful people.

Taino society was complex and well-organized, with a hierarchy of caciques or chiefs who governed different regions. They lived in large, oval-shaped houses called bohíos, made of wood and palm leaves, often built around a central plaza in the village. They grew crops like corn, yams, and cassava, and they were also skilled fishermen, navigating the Caribbean Sea in their canoes, or "caney."

They also had a rich spiritual life. The Taino believed in many gods, or "zemis", each responsible for different aspects of life. They made beautiful zemi sculptures, and some of these, preserved over centuries, give us an idea of their artistic skill.

However, the arrival of the Europeans brought disaster to the Taino. They were enslaved, forced to work in mines and plantations, and many died from European diseases against which they had no immunity. Yet, the Taino have not been entirely erased. Their legacy lives on in the language, food, and culture of the Caribbean people today.

Fun Facts

- The hammock, an iconic symbol of relaxation, was actually invented by the Taino.
- Many words we use today, like hurricane, barbecue, canoe, and even Caribbean, are of Taino origin.

The Caribs: The Warriors of the Windward Islands

Unlike the Taino, the Caribs were known for their fierceness and warrior culture. They inhabited the Lesser Antilles, especially the Windward Islands, and their reputation as warriors was so formidable that the Caribbean Sea was named after them.

Carib society was divided into two main classes: the nobles and the common people. Each village was ruled by a chief, or "ubutu", who was often a great warrior. The Caribs lived in circular huts, or "ajoupas", constructed with poles and thatched with palm leaves. They practiced agriculture, growing crops like cassava and sweet potatoes, but they were also excellent sailors and fishermen.

The Caribs were known for their seafaring skills and war canoes, or "pirogues". They used these fast, agile boats for travel, fishing, and, sometimes, warfare. Their navigation skills were so impressive that they could travel between islands, even in the darkest nights, guided only by the stars and the currents.

Like the Taino, the Caribs faced devastation with the arrival of the Europeans. They fiercely resisted European colonization, engaging in many battles with the Spanish, French, and English. Despite their resistance, they suffered from enslavement, disease, and displacement.

Today, the Carib people, their culture and traditions, continue to live on, particularly in Dominica, where there is a recognized territory, the Carib Territory (Kalinago Territory), where the descendants of the Caribs maintain their way of life.

Fun Facts

- The Caribs were so feared by the other tribes that the word "cannibal" originated from their name, though the claims of them being cannibals are widely debated among historians.
- The Carib women were skilled potters and weavers. Some of their traditional basket weaving techniques are still practiced today in the Caribbean.

How the Caribbean became a Haven for Pirates and Smugglers

The Caribbean was also a hotbed for pirates and smugglers. But why, you might ask? Several factors made the Caribbean a paradise for these outlaws.

First, the geography. The Caribbean Sea is sprinkled with islands, many of them uninhabited, providing plenty of hideouts for pirates and smugglers. Its shallow waters and hidden coves made for perfect pirate nests, places to lay low and evade the authorities.

Second, the trade. The Caribbean was a major hub for trade in the 17th and 18th centuries. Ships laden with goods from Europe, Africa, and the American colonies constantly criss crossed its waters. For pirates, these ships were floating treasure chests just waiting to be plucked.

Third, the politics. The constant wars between the European powers created a chaotic environment that pirates and smugglers could exploit. Sometimes, pirates were even employed as privateers, state-sponsored pirates, to attack and plunder enemy ships.

The Caribbean, with its mix of beauty and danger, its vast riches and shadowy figures, was the perfect setting for the age of piracy and smuggling. It was, in many ways, a pirate's paradise.

Jamaica, Barbados & the North American British Colonies: A Tale of Trade, Treasures, and Tides

Jamaica and Barbados, two jewels of the Caribbean, were among the British Empire's prized possessions in the 17th and 18th centuries. These islands weren't just famous for their tropical beauty; they were the economic powerhouses of the colonial world. But to understand their story, we also need to venture north, to the 13 American colonies.

In the warm Caribbean climate, sugarcane thrived. Plantations sprawled across Jamaica and Barbados, fueled by the grueling labor of African slaves. The sugar produced was then shipped across the Atlantic to the bustling ports of Europe. It was a bitter truth, but this "white gold" made fortunes for plantation owners and filled the British coffers.

The North American British colonies, meanwhile, were known for their production of tobacco, rice, indigo, and later, cotton.

Unlike the Caribbean colonies, where vast plantations dominated, North American colonies also had smaller farms and a more diverse economy.

Trade between these colonies was essential. North America provided food and lumber to the Caribbean colonies, while the Caribbean sent sugar, molasses, and rum to the North. This trade network was like the lifeblood of the British Empire.

However, where there's trade, pirates aren't far behind. With so many merchant ships filled with valuable goods sailing the Atlantic, the waters between the Caribbean and the North American colonies became a playground for pirates.

From hidden coves in Jamaica and Barbados, pirates would set sail to intercept and loot these merchant ships. They'd then sell the stolen goods to willing buyers, often in the very colonies where the goods were intended to go. Even though piracy was illegal, the prospect of cheaper goods (no taxes!) made many colonists turn a blind eye.

The relationship between the pirates and the colonies was complicated. On one hand, pirates were outlaws, feared and despised. On the other hand, they were often seen as rebellious heroes, fighting against the unfair trade laws imposed by the British.

Pirates like Blackbeard and Calico Jack roamed these waters, becoming legendary figures. The activities of these pirates added a layer of danger and excitement to the trade networks between Jamaica, Barbados, and the North American British colonies, forever shaping the history of this region.

And so, while these colonies grew and prospered, the shadow of the Jolly Roger never quite left the horizon. For in these waters, where trade, treasures, and tides intertwined, pirates found a home, making the Caribbean truly the Pirate's Paradise.

The Pirate Round - A Lethal Detour

The sea routes of the 17th and early 18th centuries were bustling highways of commerce, with ships of various nationalities and purposes crisscrossing the vast blue expanses. Among these were the pirates, who, like the highwaymen of old, saw the sea as their personal hunting ground. One of these sea routes, infamous among merchants and a favorite among pirates, was known as the "Pirate Round."

At first glance, the Pirate Round might appear to be a significant detour. It started in the Caribbean, known for its bustling ports and pirate havens, then stretched thousands of miles east, around the southern tip of Africa, and into the Indian Ocean, before looping back to the Caribbean. The length of the journey was daunting, but the potential reward was enough to tempt many a pirate.

Why was this route so popular among the sea brigands? The answer lies in the treasures that lay at the end of this route: the richly laden ships of the British and Dutch East India companies, as well as Muslim ships in the Indian Ocean and Red Sea. These ships were filled to the brim with goods like spices, silks, and precious metals, the sale of which generated immense wealth. For pirates, these vessels represented a potentially massive haul.

The journey to the Indian Ocean was no pleasure cruise. It required careful planning and navigating through treacherous waters, particularly around the Cape of Good Hope, the southern tip of Africa. The pirates had to avoid not only the natural dangers of the sea but also patrols of warships from various nations looking to protect their trading interests.

Once in the Indian Ocean, the pirates would lie in wait near key trading ports, ready to pounce on unsuspecting merchant vessels. The most famous of these ports was the island of Madagascar, off the southeastern coast of Africa. Its favorable location, combined with a lack of effective authority, made it an ideal base for pirates operating in the Indian Ocean.

After a successful raid, the pirates would head back to the Caribbean, their holds filled with stolen treasures. The return journey was just as perilous, if not more so, as the outbound voyage. The pirates had to avoid capture, navigate around adverse weather conditions, and sometimes even deal with mutinies among their crew. But those who made it back enjoyed a wealth and reputation few others could match.

The Pirate Round was more than just a sea route; it was a symbol of the pirates' audacity and cunning. They turned a trade route into a hunting ground, braved the dangers of the sea, and defied the might of nations for a chance at fortune and infamy. Their exploits have passed into legend, adding another chapter to the colorful history of the high seas.

The Pirate's Booty and the 13 Colonies

While the daring feats and brutal tactics of the pirates are well-known and often glamorized, their journeys would have been fruitless without a means to sell their spoils. The markets for their illicitly-gained goods were not in far-off lands but right in the heart of the original 13 colonies.

The colonists, living far from the European centers of commerce, had an appetite for goods that were otherwise difficult to obtain or were made expensive by taxes and shipping costs. The pirates' booty, which often included exotic goods from India, China, and Indonesia, filled this gap in the market.

Pirates had to be shrewd when selling their plunder. Officially, piracy was a crime punishable by death, and harboring or dealing with pirates was also considered illegal. But in practice, this wasn't always the case. Some colonists, including those in positions of authority, turned a blind eye to the pirates' activities. They recognized that the flow of goods from pirates benefited the colonies, stimulating economic growth and providing access to goods not readily available elsewhere. Therefore, it was common for pirates to bring their goods to friendly ports where local authorities were willing to ignore their illicit activities in exchange for a cut of the profits or goods.

The most well-known of these 'pirate-friendly' ports was the bustling town of Newport in the colony of Rhode Island.

Rhode Island's semi-autonomous status and its distance from the central authorities in England made it a haven for pirates returning from the Pirate Round. Rhode Island was notorious for its lax attitudes towards piracy. At one point, nearly every family in Newport was said to have been involved in the pirate trade in some way.

However, selling their booty was not as simple as walking into a market and setting up a stall. Pirates had to maintain a low profile and often relied on a network of trusted merchants, tavern keepers, and other accomplices who would buy the goods and then sell them to the general public. Some of these middlemen became wealthy in their own right, thanks to their dealings with pirates.

Despite the risk, the rewards made the Pirate Round an irresistible lure for those willing to live outside the law. Colonists often found pirate goods more affordable than the same items from legal sources, as pirates had no taxes or duties to pay. The pirates provided them a much-needed supply of goods, albeit illicitly, that contributed to the growth and prosperity of the young American colonies.

As British regulations tightened around the colonies, prohibiting or heavily taxing imports of certain goods, the temptation of smuggling only grew. Pirates, with their bounty of unregulated goods, became the perfect suppliers for colonists eager for items they couldn't legally obtain.

Many colonial ports had a thriving black market, where goods captured by pirates were sold off to eager customers. Luxury items like silk, spices, and fine wines, as well as everyday commodities like sugar and molasses, made their way into the colonies through these channels.

The colonies were often far removed from the prying eyes of British regulators, and many colonial governors chose to ignore or even participate in this underground economy. They reasoned that if the goods were going to be sold anyway, they might as well benefit their own colonies rather than foreign ports.

For instance, Benjamin Fletcher, governor of New York from 1692 to 1697, was notorious for his involvement in the pirate economy. He granted pirate ships safe harbor in New York City, allowing them to sell their stolen goods and even offering them legal protection. Fletcher was eventually recalled to England under charges of corruption and 'piracy.' However, he managed to escape punishment by convincing the authorities that he'd only been trying to boost New York's economy.

During times of conflict, like during the French and Indian War, smuggling could take on a patriotic tone. Smuggled goods often included essential supplies like gunpowder, arms, and ammunition. By purchasing these items from pirates and smugglers, colonists believed they were supporting their local militias and aiding the war effort against French and Native American forces.

The restrictions imposed by Britain and the colonists' increasing reliance on smuggled goods would ultimately fuel the revolutionary spirit that led to the American Revolution. The smuggling operations helped the colonies become economically independent from Britain and sowed the seeds of rebellion.

In this way, the pirate's booty had a significant impact on the history of the 13 colonies. The illicit goods not only enriched individuals and boosted the local economy, but they also helped ignite the flame of independence that would eventually engulf the colonies in revolution.

Fun Facts

- The term "Pirate Round" was coined by historians. During the era of piracy, it was simply known as "going on the account" or "going on the adventure." Some pirates became so successful on the Pirate Round that they retired to a life of luxury.
- Port Royal in Jamaica was known as the "wickedest city on Earth" because of its reputation as a pirate haven. After a massive earthquake in 1692, much of the city sank beneath the sea, a disaster some believed was divine punishment for its lawlessness.
- Pirates and smugglers often used the cover of darkness and the local knowledge of the Caribbean waters to their advantage. By using secret channels through the reefs that only they knew about, they could escape from pursuing naval vessels.
- Pirates had a form of 'insurance'. If a pirate was injured, he received a larger share of the loot.
- Did you know that the original recipe for rum, a drink loved by pirates, came from Barbados? In colonial times, rum was

considered good for health and was even used as a medicine.

- The Cape of Good Hope was originally named the Cape of Storms by Portuguese explorer Bartolomeu Dias due to the treacherous weather conditions.
- The Golden Age's Most Successful Pirate – The pirate to capture the most ships during the Golden Age of Piracy wasn't Blackbeard or Calico Jack, but Bartholomew "Black Bart" Roberts. In just three years, he captured an estimated 400 ships!

Chapter 6 Quiz:

1. The first people Christopher Columbus encountered in the Americas were the ______________.
2. The word "Taino" means ______________.
3. ______________ were known for their fierceness and warrior culture.
4. The Caribbean Sea was named after the ______________ people.
5. Jamaica and Barbados were among the British Empire's ______________.
6. The North American British colonies were known for their production of ______________, ______________, ______________, and ______________.
7. The waters between the Caribbean and the North American colonies became a playground for ______________.
8. Pirates like ______________ and ______________ roamed the waters between the Caribbean and the North American colonies.

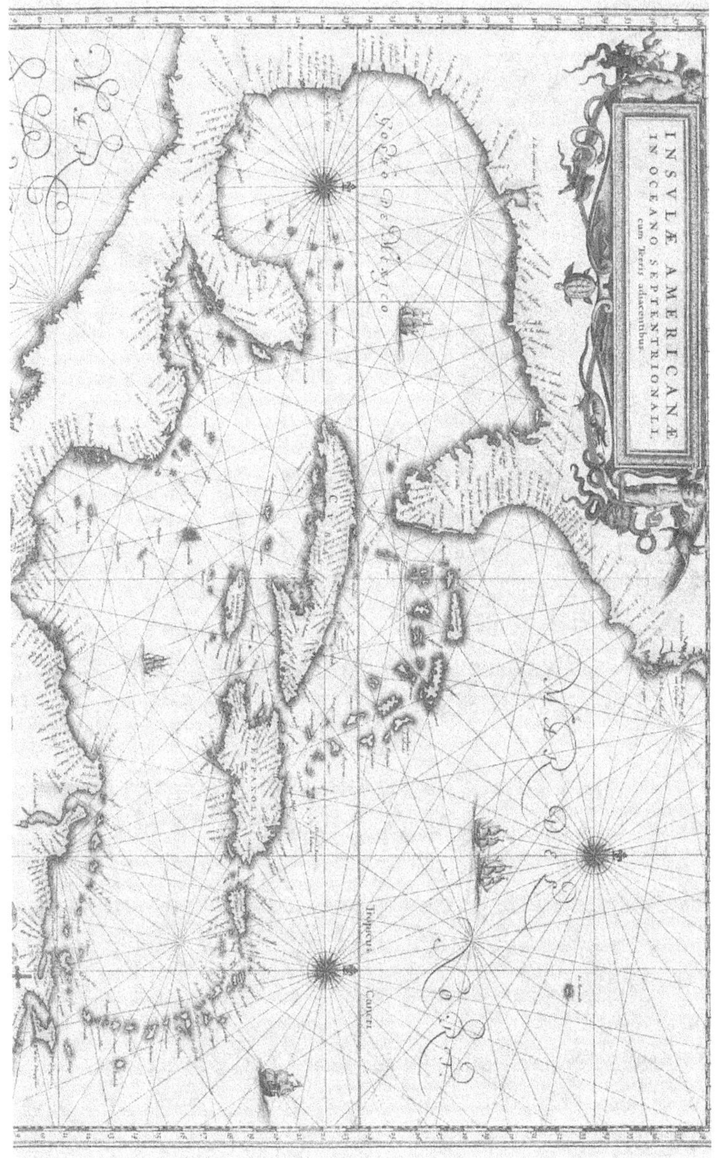

INSVLÆ AMERICANÆ
IN OCEANO SEPTENTRIONALI
cum Terris adiacentibus

Chapter Seven: Africa – The Unwilling Participant

Africa's Role in the Triangular Trade

In the great puzzle of colonial trade, Africa was a crucial piece, though often an unwilling one. This was largely due to the infamous 'Triangular Trade,' so named for the shape of the trade routes between Europe, Africa, and the Americas. Let's dive deeper into Africa's role in this pivotal part of history.

The Triangular Trade was a system where ships would carry goods from Europe to Africa, African slaves to the Americas, and then American products, particularly sugar and tobacco, back to Europe. This cycle was repeated over and over, making many Europeans very rich. Sadly, the cost was high for Africa and her people.

In Africa, coastal and near-coastal tribes were enticed or coerced by European traders into capturing people from more inland tribes. These captives were traded for European goods like cloth, guns, and alcohol, and then packed into ships and sent across the Atlantic, a journey now known as the 'Middle Passage.' Conditions on these ships were unspeakably harsh.

The Harrowing Journey – The Slave Trade and the 'Middle Passage'

The Transatlantic Slave Trade was a dark chapter in world history, and the 'Middle Passage' was one of its darkest pages. The brutal journey that millions of African men, women, and children were forced to undertake is an unfathomable tale of suffering, resilience, and, for some, survival.

To understand the magnitude of the slave trade, let's look at the numbers. From the 16th to the 19th century, historians estimate that up to 12 million African people were captured and transported across the Atlantic Ocean to work on plantations in the Americas. These human beings were not just numbers; they were people with their own cultures, families, and dreams. But to the traders, they were merely cargo, a commodity to be bought and sold for profit.

The Slave Trade was, unfortunately, a key part of the colonial economy. European traders would first travel to Africa loaded with goods like cloth, guns, alcohol, and beads. These goods were exchanged with African merchants, rulers, or raiders for captives, who were then loaded onto ships for the horrifying journey known as the 'Middle Passage.'

The conditions on these ships were unimaginably harsh. The

captives were chained together, crammed into spaces with little room to move, often forced to lie in their own filth. Disease was rampant, and death was a common occurrence. It's estimated that around 15% of Africans aboard the slave ships died during the 'Middle Passage.'

Once the ships reached the Americas, the surviving captives were sold at slave markets to the highest bidder. They were then taken to plantations where they were forced to work in grueling conditions, their freedom and dignity stripped away.

The 'Middle Passage' was a journey of unimaginable hardship, a trial of human endurance against the worst conditions. But it was also a journey of resistance and survival. Despite the odds, many African people resisted their captors, maintaining their cultures and identities, even in the face of such adversity. Their stories, too often overlooked, are a testament to the human spirit's resilience and strength.

Impact of Piracy and Smuggling on Africa

Piracy and smuggling had a profound impact on Africa during this period, though not always in ways you might expect. Pirates didn't often target African coasts for raids as they did in the Americas and the Caribbean. The African coastline was vast, less familiar, and far from their bases in the Caribbean and Atlantic islands. However, they played a role in the slave trade.

Some pirates intercepted slave ships crossing the Atlantic,

but not just to steal the gold and other goods aboard. Many pirates, especially those in the Caribbean, were escaped slaves themselves or dispossessed people who had a deep hatred for the slave trade. When they captured these ships, they often freed the captives, adding to their crews or setting up maroon communities of freed slaves in the Caribbean.

Smugglers, meanwhile, were a part of the larger system that perpetuated the slave trade. They sought to avoid paying duties and taxes on their goods, including slaves. This illicit trade not only furthered the suffering of the African people but also added more tension between the colonists and their European rulers, eventually contributing to events like the American Revolution.

The piracy and smuggling of this era left an indelible mark on Africa. Millions of its people were taken away, communities were destroyed or forever altered, and the continent was left to grapple with a legacy that still has effects to this day. Yet, amidst this tumultuous history, stories of resistance and re-silience also emerged, hinting at the spirit and strength of the African people.

The Madagascar Connection – An Unexpected Pirate Haven

Despite being located on the other side of the African continent, a large island off the southeastern coast of Africa played a surprising role in the world of colonial American piracy. This island was Madagascar, a land known for its unique wildlife and diverse cultures.

Madagascar became a pirate paradise in the late 17th century due to its strategic location. It was conveniently positioned along major sea routes from the Americas to Asia, and vice versa. It was also far enough away from European authorities for pirates to safely restock, repair their ships, and sell stolen goods.

The colonies in North America were a source of goods, crews, and, of course, targets for these pirates. Colonial merchants would often buy goods brought back by pirates from the Indian Ocean and Asia, such as spices, silk, and precious stones. They paid in colonial-produced goods or specie (gold and silver coin). The pirates would return to Madagascar, restock, and then head back out for the richly laden ships sailing from Asia to the colonies and Europe.

However, the pirate presence in Madagascar wasn't without its problems. Pirates often clashed with local Malagasy tribes and kingdoms. And as the British and other European powers increased their naval presence in the Indian Ocean, the pirate haven of Madagascar began to lose its appeal. By the mid-18th century, Madagascar was no longer the pirate utopia it once was, but its legacy in the annals of piracy and colonial trade would endure.

Piracy was not just a series of rogue operations but an intricate network spread across continents and seas, with places like Madagascar serving as important nodes. By sailing between the colonies and Madagascar, pirates were not only extending their reach but also the reach of the American colonies, linking them to far-off lands in ways that they hadn't been before. These connections would play a vital role in shaping the colonies and their future as they steered toward the revolutionary days to come.

Fascinating Facts

- Did you know that the Triangular Trade wasn't always a strict triangle? Ships often stopped at multiple ports along each route.
- Resistance aboard the slave ships was not uncommon. There were numerous recorded instances of revolts, with the captives attempting to take over the ship or jump overboard.
- Some historians believe the actual number of African people captured and transported could be much higher than 12 million, as many records were lost, destroyed, or never kept.
- Some African kings and chieftains actively fought against the slave trade. King Nzinga Mbemba Affonso of Congo was one who sent letters to the king of Portugal in the 1520s, pleading for an end to the trade.

- "Maroon" communities come from the Spanish word 'cimarrón,' which means 'wild' or 'untamed.' These were settlements formed by escaped slaves in the Caribbean, Florida, and other areas of the Americas.
- Did you know that Madagascar is the fourth largest island in the world? Its size made it an ideal base for pirates.
- Pirates loved to use Madagascar's abundant natural resources to repair and maintain their ships. The island's forests provided excellent timber.
- Some pirates even settled in Madagascar, marrying local women and creating their own pirate kingdoms.

In our next chapter, we'll explore the rising tensions between two European powers, Spain and Britain, and how their rivalries fueled the fires of piracy and smuggling.

Chapter 7 Quiz:

1. Madagascar became a pirate paradise in the late 17th century due to its ______________.
2. Some pirates settled in Madagascar and created their own ______________.
3. From the 16th to the 19th century, historians estimate that up to ______________ African people were captured and transported across the Atlantic Ocean.
4. European traders would first travel to Africa loaded with goods like cloth, guns, alcohol, and beads. These goods were exchanged with African ______________ for captives.
5. The captives were loaded onto ships for the horrifying journey known as the '______________'.

6. It's estimated that around _______________% of Africans aboard the slave ships died during the 'Middle Passage.'

7. Resistance aboard the slave ships was _______________.

8. Despite the odds, many African people resisted their captors, maintaining their _______________ and identities.

Chapter Eight: The Spanish & British – Unlikely Catalysts

Overview of the Spanish and British Relationship

Spain and Britain were two of the most formidable powers in Europe during the period of colonial America. At the time, both nations had vast, resource-rich colonies across the globe, and their influence was felt in every corner of the world. However, their relationship was marred by frequent conflict and intense rivalry. In the 16th and 17th centuries, Spain and Britain were rivals in everything from global exploration to trade and even religion. This rivalry was often heated and spilled over into open warfare.

Spain was the first to establish a large and prosperous colonial empire in the New World, beginning with the voyages of Christopher Columbus in 1492. The immense wealth pouring into Spain from its American colonies, particularly silver and gold, made it the envy of Europe. At its height, the Spanish Empire was one of the largest the world had ever seen. It stretched across the Americas, from California to Patagonia, and included parts of Europe, Africa, and Asia.

Britain, meanwhile, was a latecomer to the colonial race. Its first permanent colony in the New World, Jamestown, wasn't established until 1607, over a century after Columbus's first voyage. However, Britain quickly made up for lost time, establishing colonies across North America and the Caribbean and becoming a dominant force in global trade. Many of the original 13 colonies, including Virginia (home of Jamestown), were named after British monarchs or places in Britain.

Despite their global reach, or perhaps because of it, Spain and Britain were constantly at odds. Disputes over territory, trade, and religious differences frequently led to wars and skirmishes both at home and in their colonies. From 1650 to 1780, Spain and Britain were officially at war seven times. These wars often had dramatic effects on the American colonies.

How Their Rivalry Fuelled Piracy and Smuggling

The constant conflict between Spain and Britain had an unexpected consequence: it spurred the growth of piracy and smuggling, particularly in the American colonies and the Caribbean. During periods of war, both countries frequently used privateers—essentially state-sanctioned pirates—to attack each other's ships and disrupt trade.

Privateering was a lucrative venture for both the state and the privateers themselves. These mariners were given a license, known as a letter of marque, that allowed them to attack and plunder enemy vessels during times of war. This was a boon for England, as privateers bolstered the navy's ranks and helped wage economic warfare against Spain.

Pirate or Privateer? – Temptation on the High Seas

When peace was declared, privateers were expected to return to a life of normal seafaring. But the lure of easy wealth was too strong for many, and they continued their piratical activities. When wars ended, privateers often became pirates, as the skills and tactics used in privateering—such as navigation, raiding, and combat—were easily transferable to piracy.

Spain's vast wealth was a constant target for pirates. Spanish galleons loaded with gold, silver, and precious goods from the New World sailed regularly across the Atlantic, a tempting target for any sea rover. These routes became known as the Spanish Main, a magnet for pirates and privateers. The Spanish treasure fleets were such a favorite target of pirates that they began to travel in large convoys for protection.

The rivalry also fuelled smuggling. England, eager to keep the wealth of its colonies within its own economy, imposed strict trade laws known as the Navigation Acts. These laws were designed to undercut Spain's dominance and keep English colonies from trading with other nations. However, they were unpopular in the colonies and difficult to enforce.

The Navigation Acts were one of the key grievances that eventually led to the American Revolution. As a result, smuggling became a common practice in the colonies. Merchants would illegally trade goods with other nations, often at night or in secluded coves to avoid detection.

The Effects on the American Colonies

The rivalry between Spain and Britain had profound effects on the American colonies. This was not just in terms of the overall colonial economy, but it also impacted day-to-day life and even played a role in shaping the future United States.

The colonial era was a time of great change and uncertainty in America. Conflicts between Spain and Britain played a significant role in shaping these colonies, both economically and socially.

As mentioned, one of the key results of the rivalry was the Navigation Acts imposed by Britain. These laws stipulated that colonial goods could only be shipped on English ships and sold primarily to English markets. This was designed to ensure that the wealth of the colonies stayed within the British Empire and didn't benefit Spain or other rival powers.

The Navigation Acts not only limited who the colonists could trade with, but they also dictated what they could produce. Certain goods, such as tobacco and sugar, could only be grown for export to England, not for sale within the colonies.

However, these restrictions were hugely unpopular in the colonies and led to widespread smuggling. Many colonial merchants, seeing the potential for greater profits elsewhere, chose to trade illegally with other nations, including Spain and France. Colonial smuggling was so widespread that Benjamin Franklin once claimed that no one in the colonies ever obeyed the Navigation Acts.

The constant wars between Spain and Britain also brought turmoil and disruption to the colonies. Battles often spilled over into colonial territory, leading to lost trade, destruction of property, and even loss of life. In response, many colonists took up arms to defend their homes and livelihoods.

Meanwhile, the lure of plunder and the thrill of defying authority made piracy and privateering attractive to many colonists. Some, like William Kidd and Blackbeard, even achieved infamy for their deeds. Many colonial governors were rumored to have colluded with pirates. For example, Governor Thomas Modyford of Jamaica was another well-known example of a colonial governor involved in piracy and smuggling. His tenure was in the 17th century, a peak period for piracy.

Modyford had a notorious relationship with pirates, particularly with the infamous Captain Henry Morgan. While serving as governor of Jamaica, Modyford regularly turned a blind eye to Morgan's piratical actions, and in many cases, he even provided the buccaneer with official papers authorizing his raids on Spanish settlements. These "commissions" were technically for privateering, but they were commonly understood to be licenses for piracy.

Modyford's leniency and support of piracy were driven in part by his own greed—he himself had invested in several privateering ventures—and also by the overall strategic benefits to the British Empire. The activities of pirates and privateers like Morgan served to undermine Spain's power and influence in the Caribbean and, at the same time, boosted Jamaica's economy, which largely depended on the trade of goods taken from Spanish ships and settlements.

Modyford was eventually recalled to England and briefly imprisoned because of his association with Morgan. However, the British government soon released him, recognizing the value of his aggressive strategy against the Spanish in the Caribbean. This episode serves as an example of how intricate and controversial the relationship between colonial authorities and pirates could be. It also shows how politics and piracy affected life in the colonies from down in Jamaica all the way to New England.

Perhaps the most lasting effect of the Spanish-British rivalry was how it stoked the flames of discontent in the colonies. The Navigation Acts and other restrictive policies led to resentment among colonists, who felt their rights and opportunities were being suppressed for the benefit of far-off England.

The American Revolution was driven by many factors, but one key aspect was resentment against British economic policies. The slogan "No taxation without representation" became a rallying cry for colonists demanding greater economic freedom.

In this way, the rivalry between Spain and Britain contributed to the birth of the United States. While they may have been unintended, these consequences shaped the course of history and continue to be felt to this day.

Chapter 8 Quiz:

1. The _____________ and _____________ had an intense rivalry during the colonial era, fueling piracy and smuggling.
2. The Spanish and British rivalry had major effects on the _____________ colonies.
3. _____________ was a notorious colonial governor of New York known for his involvement in the pirate economy.
4. The _____________ and Indian War was a time when smuggling took on a patriotic tone.
5. Restrictions imposed by Britain and the reliance on smuggled goods fueled the _____________ spirit in the American colonies.

Chapter Nine: The Golden Age of Piracy

Pirates at Their Peak

Imagine a time when pirate flags adorned the masts of countless ships, a time when the Jolly Roger struck fear into the hearts of sailors and settlers alike. This period, often called the 'Golden Age of Piracy,' was no mere invention of storybooks or movies, but a real era of history, teeming with danger, adventure, and of course, lots and lots of pirates.

From around 1650 to 1730, piracy was at its peak. It was an age where pirates ruled the waves and became legends, their names whispered in taverns and on ship decks from the Caribbean to the coastlines of Africa. But what made this period so 'golden' for piracy?

The term 'Golden Age of Piracy' is a phrase used by historians to describe a period in the late 17th and early 18th centuries when piracy was particularly rampant. Many factors came together during this era to create the perfect storm for piracy. The ending of the War of Spanish Succession had left many sailors jobless and penniless. With no prospects on land, many turned to the sea's lawless frontier. Additionally, the rise in overseas trade presented countless opportunities for pirates to strike it rich. These were just some of the elements that set the stage for the Golden Age of Piracy.

This was a time of daring high-seas robbery, of fierce battles, and escapes that were too unbelievable to be made up. The pirate ships of this era were their own miniature kingdoms, ruled not by kings and queens but by captains and quartermasters. Pirate crews lived by their own laws and codes, in stark contrast to the harsh discipline and low pay of the navy and merchant vessels.

The Golden Age of Piracy was not only a time of terror but also of fascination. It was an age that inspired countless stories, from childhood tales to novels, music, and films, shaping our perception of piracy and this time period for centuries to come. The modern conception of pirates as depicted in popular culture is derived largely, although not always accurately, from the Golden Age of Piracy.

Let's meet more of this era's infamous pirates...

From Nobility to Notoriety: The Treacherous Transformation of William Kidd

William Kidd was one of the most famous privateers turned pirates in history. Also known as Captain Kidd, he was born in Scotland around 1645. In his early career, he was considered a reputable privateer, commissioned by the English government. He was known for his seafaring skills, and by the 1690s, Kidd was living in New York and was a respected member of society, even marrying a wealthy widow.

In 1695, Kidd received a privateering commission from King William III of England to hunt down pirates operating in the Indian Ocean. The mission was also to harass French ships, as England and France were enemies at the time. Kidd set sail on the ship "Adventure Galley" with a crew of about 150 men.

However, the line between privateering and piracy was often thin and blurry. Unable to find the pirates he was commissioned to hunt, and facing a mutinous crew desperate for booty, Kidd's mission dramatically changed course. Kidd began attacking ships not covered under his commission, effectively turning into a pirate.

One of the most infamous incidents involved the capture of an Armenian ship, the "Quedagh Merchant," which was carrying a valuable cargo and was captained by an Englishman but was sailing under a French pass. Kidd argued that the French pass made it a legitimate target, but the English authorities did not agree.

Kidd returned to New York in 1699, hoping to resolve the charges against him. Legend has it that he buried treasure along the way. Four locations in New Jersey stand out among the numerous that have been suggested as the potential locations for Kidd's lost riches.

One location is Cape May, which was frequently visited by pirate ships as a source of freshwater. An island at the entrance of the Toms River, which offered refuge from ocean storms to pirates, is another potential location. Sandy Hook, close to where Kidd moored on his last trip in Raritan Bay, is a third location.

The location of the most well-known and likely burial was probably around Sandy Hook, close to Whales (Wales) Creek. A little island off the coast is where several Spanish gold coins from the 17th century were discovered.

While traveling to Boston in June 1699 to face pirate accusations, he also made a stop at Gardiner's Island, New York. He buried treasure chests in a ravine with the owner of the island's consent.

Governor Bellomont of Massachusetts told Gardiner to bring the wealth as evidence when Kidd was put on trial in Boston. Gold dust, silver bars, Spanish dollars, rubies, jewels, and candlesticks were among the loot. The location of the treasure's burial is designated by a plaque on the island.

Kidd was sent to England for trial. Despite his insistence that he had not turned pirate, Kidd was found guilty and hanged in 1701. After his execution, Kidd's tarred body was hung in a cage over the River Thames for three years as a warning to would-be pirates. William Kidd's story is a dramatic example of the perilous and often morally ambiguous life of a privateer in the age of colonial empires.

Plunder under Thunder: The Daring Raid of Black Sam Bellamy and the Whydah's Lost Treasure

During the first half of the eighteenth century, "Black Sam" Bellamy, an English seaman turned pirate. He is most famous for being the richest pirate in history and an exemplar of the Golden Age of Piracy. He and his men managed to capture at least 53 ships despite the fact that his known career as a pirate commander lasted only a little over a year.

Bellamy, known as "Black Sam" in Cape Cod mythology for forgoing the trendy powdered wig in favor of tying back his long black hair with a band, rose to fame for his charity and mercy toward people he seized during his raids. He also acquired the nickname "Prince of Pirates" as a result of his leniency. He compared himself to Robin Hood, and his group was known as "Robin Hood's Men."

In his adolescent years, Bellamy, who was born in Devon, England, started sailing for the British Royal Navy. He traveled to Cape Cod around 1715, then went south to Florida trying to locate a sunken treasure fleet. From there, he traveled to the Bahamas while being commanded by Edward "Blackbeard" Teach and Benjamin Hornigold. After Hornigold and Teach were voted out of command, Bellamy took a captured vessel as his own pirate ship. His pirate career got off to a fast start, and one huge heist stood out for all time.

In the annals of pirate lore, few tales are as thrilling as the audacious high-seas robbery orchestrated by the notorious "Black Sam" Bellamy in 1717. Known for his democratic leadership and for being called the 'Robin Hood of the Sea,' Bellamy's greatest triumph came with the capture of the grand ship, the "Whydah Gally."

The Whydah began its life as a slave ship, commissioned by Sir Humphrey Morice, a prominent London merchant. After a successful maiden voyage transporting enslaved Africans from West Africa to the Caribbean, the Whydah was laden with a rich trove of sugar, indigo, Jesuit's bark, ivory, and gold, set to return to England. It was this treasure-laden ship that caught the eye of Bellamy and his crew.

The chase began on the evening of April 26, 1717, off the coast of Cape Cod. As Bellamy's ship, the 'Sultana', drew near, the Whydah's captain, Lawrence Prince, tried to evade capture by steering his ship into a coming storm. Prince was a seasoned captain and hoped the weather would deter the pirates. But Bellamy was undeterred.

Through the howling winds and massive waves, Bellamy's ship relentlessly pursued the Whydah. The chase lasted into the early hours of the next day. Under the cover of the stormy darkness, Bellamy's men crept onto the Whydah and seized control of the ship with minimal resistance.

In the end, the grand Whydah was overtaken, and Bellamy claimed the ship as his own, moving his flag onto the Whydah. The treasures within the Whydah were beyond their wildest dreams: over 4.5 tons of gold, silver, and other goods, an unimaginable fortune for the time.

In a surprising act of mercy, Bellamy gave the defeated Captain Prince his older, lesser ship, the 'Sultana.' This act of *kindness* was less about compassion and more about adding insult to injury. It was as though Bellamy was saying, "I'm taking your grand ship and leaving you with my lesser one."

Word of Bellamy's audacious raid spread through the colonies, amplifying his already infamous reputation. Yet, his triumph was short-lived. Just weeks later, the Whydah was swept up in another storm, this one far more vicious. Laden with its stolen treasure, the Whydah sank off the coast of Cape Cod, taking Bellamy and most of his crew down with it. The Whydah Gally was the first completely confirmed Golden Age pirate ship discovered in North America when her wreckage was found in 1984.

The story of Bellamy and the Whydah's raid remains one of the most audacious heists of the Golden Age of Piracy. It encapsulates the lure of the sea and the unfathomable riches it promised, the dangers it posed, and the swift, merciless justice it could sometimes serve. It's a tale of fortune, audacity, and a stark reminder of the perilous, fleeting life of a pirate in colonial America.

Legends Among Thieves

Now that we understand the broader strokes of the Golden Age of Piracy, let's take a closer look at some of the individuals who defined this era. After all, what is a golden age without its shining stars?

Take, for example the pirates we've already discussed, the infamous Edward Teach, better known as Blackbeard. Blackbeard was a towering figure, both in physical size and reputation. He is said to have lit slow-burning fuses in his beard during battles, creating a terrifying image of a man wreathed in smoke and flame. His ship, the Queen Anne's Revenge, was a formidable sight on the seas.

Then there was the audacious William Kidd, or Captain Kidd, as he was better known. Kidd began his career as a privateer but was later accused of turning pirate. His trial and subsequent execution sparked debate at the time about the legality and morality of piracy and privateering.

Not all notorious pirates were men. Anne Bonny and Mary Read were two female pirates who sailed under the command of Calico Jack Rackham. They were known for their fierce fighting skills and their refusal to abide by societal expectations for women.

These figures, larger than life and twice as daring, have become the faces of the Golden Age of Piracy. They lived lives of high risk and high reward, forever sailing on the edge of danger.

Rogues of the Seas: Calico Jack, Anne Bonny and Mary Read

Our story begins with a man known as Calico Jack Rackham, named so because of the calico clothing he wore. Jack was a pirate captain who operated in the West Indies during the Golden Age of Piracy Among his crew were two of the most famed women in pirate history: Anne Bonny and Mary Read.

Calico Jack started his career as a quartermaster under the notorious pirate Charles Vane. Rackham was a brash man with a love for flamboyant clothing and daring exploits. He took over Vane's command when Vane showed 'cowardice in the face of the enemy' during an encounter with a French man-of-war. After seizing control, Rackham and his crew of buccaneers prowled the Caribbean Sea, raiding merchant ships for their goods and valuables.

It was during a stint in Nassau, a known pirate haven, that Jack met Anne Bonny. Bonny, the fiery redhead, was the wife of a small-time pirate turned informant, but she was far from a dutiful wife. She was known for her temper and was as comfortable in a tavern brawl as any man. Bonny was captivated by Rackham's audacious nature, and Rackham was equally taken by her spirit. She left her husband to join Rackham aboard his ship.

As if having one female pirate wasn't unusual enough, Rackham's crew boasted another in the form of Mary Read. Read had been disguised as a boy by her mother since childhood and had even served in the British military before turning to piracy.

She joined Rackham's crew and formed a close bond with Anne Bonny.

The trio of Rackham, Bonny, and Read created quite a name for themselves in the pirate-infested waters of the Caribbean. They led numerous successful raids and were known for their brazen attacks and flamboyant style. Yet, they were also seen as a symbol of rebellion and freedom, openly flouting the norms of the time.

One of their most daring exploits occurred when they boldly attacked a Spanish galleon loaded with treasures off the coast of Jamaica. Despite being outnumbered, they managed to board the galleon and overpower the crew, making off with a hefty haul of gold, silver, and other valuable goods.

But the life of a pirate is not all adventure and riches. There are perils and consequences. In October 1720, Rackham's ship was attacked by a pirate hunter's ship commissioned by the Governor of Jamaica. The male members of the crew, including Rackham, were below deck, too drunk to fight. The defense of the ship fell to Bonny, Read, and another crew member who were the only ones able to put up resistance.

Despite their valiant fight, they were overwhelmed, and the crew was captured and taken to Jamaica. Rackham and his crew were tried and sentenced to hang for their crimes. Calico Jack's last request was to see Anne Bonny one last time, to which she famously replied, "I'm sorry to see you here, Jack, but if you had fought like a man, you would not have been hanged like a dog."

Anne Bonny and Mary Read's fate took a different turn. Both claimed to be pregnant at their trial, and because English law forbade the execution of pregnant women, they were given a stay of execution. Read died in prison, most likely due to fever or complications from childbirth. As for Anne Bonny, her fate remains a mystery.

Waves of Influence

Piracy during the Golden Age had far-reaching effects on the American colonies and their economies. Pirates played a complex role in colonial society. They were feared as lawless criminals, yet the goods they smuggled were often welcomed.

Piracy disrupted trade routes, forcing merchants to pay higher insurance and causing prices to skyrocket. Pirates' attacks made the seas treacherous, and their power on the waves disrupted the colonies' economic lifelines. Yet, at the same time, these pirates brought in goods from around the world, some of which were not available through legal channels due to British trade restrictions.

Piracy during the Golden Age was not just about treasure maps and X-marks-the-spot. It was a critical element of the colonial world, from its economy to its international relations. While the colonists may have feared the sight of a pirate ship on the horizon, they also depended on these sea rovers for their connection to the wider world. Pirates were not just thieves of the high seas; they were agents of change in a rapidly evolving world.

The Golden Age of Piracy was a time of flamboyant characters, thrilling adventures, and profound impacts. It was an era of chaos and opportunity, of danger and daring. And while the pirate's life may not have been as glamorous as it is often portrayed in fiction, there is no denying the allure and influence of these sea-faring outlaws in shaping the colonial era.

Chapter 9 Quiz:

1. One of the most famous pirates of this era was ____________, known for his flamboyant attire and his female crew members.
2. One way pirates affected the colonial economy was by ____________.
3. The notorious pirate Charles Vane was overthrown by his quartermaster ____________, who then became a pirate captain himself.
4. Anne Bonny and Mary Read were unique among pirates because they were ____________.
5. The pirate hunter who captured Calico Jack's crew was commissioned by the Governor of ____________.
6. ____________ claimed to be pregnant during her trial, which saved her from being executed.
7. One of the key reasons for the increase in piracy during the Golden Age was the end of the ____________.

Chapter Ten: The Fall of Piracy and Smuggling

Measures taken by authorities to curb piracy & smuggling

While pirates and smugglers had enjoyed their golden era, change was on the horizon. The authorities, particularly in Britain and colonial America, had grown weary of the lawless seas and were determined to bring them under control. As our story moves into the twilight of the era of piracy and smuggling, it is clear that the actions of lawmakers and military personnel had a significant impact on the decline of these activities.

One of the first and most impactful strategies employed by the authorities was the imposition of harsher laws and penalties for piracy. This era witnessed the enactment of the Piracy Act of 1717 by the British government. The Act extended the law of England to the high seas, meaning that suspected pirates could be arrested in any place, not just within the territory of the British Empire. This law also allowed pirates to be tried in "vice-admiralty courts," which were military tribunals that did not require juries and were known for their swift and often brutal justice. Pirates found guilty were usually sentenced to death by hanging.

Furthermore, the authorities began to crack down on the colonies that had been all too willing to turn a blind eye to pirate activities. Governors, like Woodes Rogers in the Bahamas, were installed with the specific mandate of eradicating piracy. Rogers famously declared in 1718, "I am come hither to extinguish all Pirates," and he largely succeeded. His combination of offering pardons to pirates who surrendered and harshly punishing those who continued their lawless ways was a turning point in the war against piracy.

Parallel to the legal actions were increases in naval patrols, specifically around piracy hotspots in the Caribbean and off the coast of colonial America. Britain significantly boosted its naval presence and established new bases to better respond to pirate attacks. These measures made piracy a much riskier, and consequently, less attractive profession.

Regarding smuggling, Britain attempted to curb this through the Navigation Acts. These laws were designed to control trade between England and its colonies and to prevent smuggling by requiring that all goods transported to and from the colonies be carried on English or colonial ships. But, this law only made colonists angry and was one of many reasons leading up to the Revolutionary War.

Effect on the colonies and Europe

The measures taken by the authorities to end piracy and smuggling had far-reaching effects on both the colonies and Europe.

In the colonies, the decline of piracy and smuggling marked a significant change. It led to the development of a more structured and law-abiding society as the colonial economies became less reliant on the black market and more integrated with legal trade. However, the removal of smuggling as a way to evade heavy British taxes played a part in stoking the flames of discontent that would eventually lead to the Revolutionary War.

The increased law enforcement on the seas also opened up new opportunities for legitimate trade and travel. Merchant ships could make their journeys with a lesser fear of pirate attacks, which in turn led to an increase in the volume of trade and contributed to the prosperity of the colonial and European economies.

In Europe, the decline of piracy and smuggling reinforced the power and control of the national governments. This increased control over their colonial territories also made colonial administration more straightforward, making it easier to impose and collect taxes and to control trade to their benefit.

However, while the golden age of piracy and smuggling came to an end, these activities did not disappear completely. They continued to persist on a smaller scale, adapting to the changes and finding new ways and areas in which to operate. And even today, tales of these daring pirates and cunning smugglers continue to captivate us, providing a fascinating glimpse into a tumultuous and colorful chapter in our history.

Overview of Efforts by Naval Forces & Colonial Authorities to Suppress Piracy

The tide began to turn against pirates in the early 18th century as naval forces and colonial authorities in Europe and the Americas launched aggressive campaigns to suppress piracy. The British Royal Navy led the charge, deploying more ships to patrol known pirate-infested waters in the Caribbean and off the coast of North America. The British also took the fight to the pirates' own lairs, raiding infamous pirate nests like New Providence in the Bahamas.

However, it wasn't just the British. The Spanish, Dutch, and French also increased their efforts to crack down on piracy, motivated not just by the loss of valuable cargo, but also by the rising political instability that piracy was causing in their colonies. Increased patrols, better organized naval strategies, and military expeditions against pirate bases were all part of the tactics used by these nations.

Meanwhile, colonial authorities, who had often turned a blind eye to piracy due to the economic benefits, were now feeling the pressure from their European overlords to take action. Governors were instructed to reject pirate goods, hang captured pirates, and hunt down the pirate crews still at large.

Strategies employed to capture or eliminate pirates

To capture or eliminate pirates, authorities used a range of strategies. Naval patrols were increased, particularly in areas where pirate attacks were frequent. New naval bases were also established to aid in rapid deployment against pirates. The British, in particular, made use of fast, heavily armed sloops that could match the pirate ships in speed and maneuverability.

Authorities also offered rewards or bounties for the capture of pirates, turning bounty hunting into a lucrative profession. Another tactic was the use of "pirate hunters" - individuals or crews specifically tasked with tracking down and capturing pirates. These hunters were often former privateers who had the knowledge and experience to take on the pirates.

Perhaps the most controversial strategy was the offering of pardons to pirates who surrendered. This policy, implemented by Woodes Rogers among others, aimed to break up pirate crews and reintegrate former pirates back into lawful society.

Profiles of Prominent Pirate Hunters

As the Golden Age of Piracy was reaching its zenith, several figures rose to prominence in the fight against piracy. While it's often the pirates themselves who become the stuff of legend, it is important to remember those who took up arms against them.

Privateer Turned Colonial Governor

Woodes Rogers, a former privateer, was appointed as the Governor of the Bahamas in 1718 with a specific mandate: eliminate piracy. Rogers arrived in New Providence, a notorious pirate haven, with a royal pardon offer for any pirate willing to surrender. Many pirates accepted the pardon, but those who resisted met a brutal end. His relentless pursuit of pirates, as well as his efforts to reform the colony, brought law and order to the Bahamas.

Benjamin Hornigold - From Pirate King to Pirate Hunter

At the height of his pirate career, Benjamin Hornigold was one of the most feared men on the high seas. He commanded a fleet of ships and had a notorious pirate named Edward Teach, better known as Blackbeard, as one of his lieutenants. Hornigold's reign as a pirate king, however, didn't last.

In 1717, King George I issued a proclamation offering clemency to any pirate who surrendered to a governor of the colonies. Hornigold was one of those who took up the offer. He renounced his pirate life and sought a pardon from the Governor of the Bahamas, Woodes Rogers. But Hornigold didn't stop there. He saw an opportunity for a new start and decided to switch sides completely. He became a pirate hunter.

The former pirate used his intimate knowledge of pirate tactics and the local waters to hunt down his former brethren. He was especially ruthless when it came to hunting down pirates who had refused the King's pardon. One of the pirates he hunted was Charles Vane, an old rival who had taken over Hornigold's command after his departure. Hornigold was relentless in his pursuit and was instrumental in driving many pirates out of the Caribbean.

Captain Robert Maynard - The End of Blackbeard

Captain Robert Maynard was a lieutenant in the British Royal Navy when he received orders to hunt down one of the most infamous pirates of all time, Blackbeard. Maynard, an experienced naval officer, was just the man for the job. His understanding of naval warfare and the mind of a pirate made him an effective hunter of these outlaws of the sea.

In November 1718, Maynard led an expedition against Blackbeard near Ocracoke Island, North Carolina. He commanded two sloops, the Jane and the Ranger, manned by a crew largely made up of volunteers. The battle that ensued was one of the fiercest in the history of pirate hunting.

Blackbeard's ship, the Adventure, had a crew of about 20 men, far fewer than Maynard's force of around 60 men. Despite the odds, Blackbeard and his crew put up a ferocious fight. The pirates managed to disable the Ranger early in the fight, forcing Maynard to continue the battle with just the Jane. Maynard used a cunning trick to lure Blackbeard in, pretending to retreat below decks. As Blackbeard and his men boarded the seemingly deserted ship, Maynard and his crew emerged from hiding, launching a surprise attack.

In the brutal hand-to-hand combat that followed, Maynard and Blackbeard crossed swords, with Blackbeard landing several blows on Maynard. But just as it looked like the pirate might win, one of Maynard's crew members came up behind Blackbeard and slashed his throat. The crew then overwhelmed the remaining pirates, bringing the bloody battle to an end. Blackbeard's reign of terror was over, thanks to Maynard's brave and strategic maneuvering.

However, victory came at a great cost. Maynard lost many men in the battle, and both his ships were severely damaged. This ferocious battle marked a turning point in the war against piracy, demonstrating the British Navy's determination to end the pirate menace.

The Battle of Ocracoke Inlet was more than a daring encounter between pirates and the British Navy; it was a symbol of the changing times. Blackbeard's defeat signaled the end of an era, as the Golden Age of Piracy started to wane, and the rule of law began to take hold in the New World.

An Unexpected Standoff: Bartholomew Roberts versus HMS Swallow

One of the most exhilarating stories of battles between pirates and the British Navy involves the legendary pirate Bartholomew Roberts, also known as Black Bart. He was reputed to be the most successful pirate of the Golden Age of Piracy, having captured over 400 ships in his career. However, his reign came to a dramatic end in a confrontation with HMS Swallow, a

British man-of-war, in February 1722.

Bartholomew Roberts wasn't your typical pirate. Unlike his foul-mouthed, hard-drinking comrades, Roberts was a teetotaler who preferred tea over rum and enforced a strict code of conduct aboard his ship, the Royal Fortune. But his gentlemanly ways didn't make him any less formidable. His strategic mind and fearless demeanor had earned him a reputation that struck terror into the hearts of sailors across the Atlantic and beyond.

The British, growing increasingly frustrated with Roberts' continuous raids, sent Captain Chaloner Ogle and his ship, HMS Swallow, to hunt down and capture the elusive pirate. Ogle was an experienced naval officer, known for his strategic acumen and tenacious spirit. He was tasked with one of the most challenging missions: ending the reign of the pirate king, Bartholomew Roberts.

In early 1722, Captain Ogle discovered Roberts anchored in Cape Lopez, off the coast of Gabon in West Africa. However, instead of attacking immediately, Ogle chose a more strategic approach. He observed the pirates from a distance, studying their habits, movements, and daily routines.

After gathering enough information, Ogle decided to strike. On February 10, 1722, under the veil of early morning mist, HMS Swallow moved into attack position. The pirates were caught by surprise. A fierce battle ensued, with cannon fire echoing across the calm sea, but the well-disciplined Royal Navy sailors managed to overwhelm the pirate crew. Bartholomew Roberts, the feared pirate, was killed by grapeshot in the initial onslaught.

However, even with their leader gone, the pirates didn't surrender easily. The battle raged on, with the remaining pirates putting up a fierce resistance. It wasn't until the late afternoon that the pirates finally admitted defeat and surrendered. Over 270 pirates were captured, marking a significant victory for the Royal Navy.

The defeat of Bartholomew Roberts was a turning point in the war against piracy. His death sent shockwaves through the pirate world and served as a stern reminder of the might of the British Navy. The capture of Roberts' crew led to one of the largest pirate trials of the time, further signifying the end of tolerance for pirates.

The standoff between HMS Swallow and Bartholomew Roberts was not just a battle; it was a clash between law and lawlessness, order and chaos, the old world and the new. This dramatic event marked a significant milestone in the struggle to end piracy and establish the rule of law in the New World.

The stories of these pirate hunters serve as fascinating glimpses into a time when the world was battling the scourge of piracy. Their experiences offer a compelling look at the struggles, tactics, and victories of those tasked with eliminating piracy from the waters of the New World. These men weren't just fighting pirates; they were shaping the future of the Americas, paving the way for the nations we know today.

The decline of piracy in colonial America

In colonial America, the decline of piracy had a significant impact. With the suppression of piracy, shipping routes became safer and trade flourished. This brought about an economic boom in many of the colonies, particularly those like New York and Massachusetts, which had significant maritime trade.

However, the decline of piracy also meant the end of easy access to goods that had previously been available through the black market. This led to increased tensions between the colonies and their European rulers, who imposed stricter trade regulations and higher taxes to maximize their profits from colonial trade.

The fall of piracy and smuggling marked the end of an era in colonial America. It heralded a shift from a rough-and-tumble, somewhat lawless society to a more organized and regulated one, setting the stage for the social and political changes that were to come in the following decades.

Chapter 10 Quiz:

1. King George I issued a proclamation in 1717 offering __________ to any pirate who surrendered to a governor of the colonies.
2. Benjamin Hornigold was a former __________ who turned into a pirate hunter after receiving a pardon.
3. One of the pirates that Hornigold hunted was __________, who took over his command after he left the life of piracy.
4. Captain Robert Maynard was a lieutenant in the __________ when he received orders to hunt down Blackbeard.

5. Maynard led an expedition against Blackbeard near __________ Island, North Carolina.
6. In their final battle, Blackbeard was finally defeated and killed, putting an end to his reign of __________.

Chapter Eleven: Pirates, Smugglers, and Revolutionaries – A Shared Spirit?

The Scent of Rebellion: Piracy, Smuggling, and the Spirit of Independence

A dramatic and unintended consequence of the era of piracy and smuggling from 1650 into the 1770s was the sense of defiance and rebellion it infused into the American colonies. The echoes of this sentiment are believed by some historians to have contributed to the revolution that later took place.

In the 18th century, British rule was very much the lifeblood of the original 13 colonies. However, a subtle undercurrent of resistance, spurred by the prohibitive Navigation Acts, was gradually brewing. These Acts, designed to protect the commercial interests of the motherland, were not well received by the colonists. The economic restrictions they imposed created a fertile ground for smuggling activities.

Smugglers, in their resistance to British economic control,

may have unintentionally fostered a sense of independence among the American colonies. Smuggling became a profitable venture, providing economic opportunities and freedom that were otherwise stifled by British rule. These economic freedoms could have planted the seeds for a broader aspiration for political and social independence.

In a similar vein, pirates demonstrated a blatant disregard for authority. They lived by their own rules, in stark contrast to the strict societal structure of the 18th century. Pirates formed their own communities, with their own codes of conduct. They were truly democratic, choosing their captains by popular vote, and distributing plunder equally. This spirit of independence and democracy was likely not lost on the American colonists.

Even though pirates were considered outlaws, some colonial governors were known to have provided them with safe harbor, effectively endorsing their defiance of British authority. This shared contempt for British rules and laws could have fueled the revolutionary spirit among the colonies.

Parallels of Defiance: Pirates, Smugglers, and Revolutionaries

The parallels between the defiance shown by pirates, smugglers, and the revolutionaries are too striking to be ignored. Pirates, smugglers, and revolutionaries all found themselves at odds with a powerful authority they felt was overbearing or unjust.

Pirates and smugglers lived by their own codes, flouting the authority of the British Empire, and their actions were a direct challenge to the established order. They not only defied the crown's economic policies but also its authority on the high seas. Pirates formed their own egalitarian societies and operated outside the strict class-based system of the period.

Revolutionaries, too, challenged the status quo. They felt the British crown was overreaching its power and imposing unfair taxes on the American colonies without their consent. Just as pirates and smugglers had done, the revolutionaries chose to defy the British authority.

Interestingly, the Sons of Liberty, an organization that played a significant role in the lead-up to the Revolutionary War, employed tactics similar to pirates and smugglers. They organized protests, disrupted British trade, and resisted taxation. The Boston Tea Party, one of the most famous acts of defiance leading up to the Revolution, was essentially an act of smuggling, with protesters dressed as Mohawk Indians throwing crates of tea into Boston Harbor to evade the tea tax.

While it might be a stretch to say that pirates and smugglers directly inspired the Revolutionary War, the spirit of defiance they embodied resonated with the colonies' burgeoning desire for self-rule. Their resistance to British authority, coupled with their pursuit of freedom – however lawless – likely echoed within the hearts and minds of the American colonists, perhaps playing a role in shaping the indomitable spirit that would soon birth a new nation.

However, it is essential to note that the idea of drawing parallels between pirates, smugglers, and revolutionaries is a somewhat romanticized notion. The reality was much more complex, and the revolutionaries were not fighting merely for personal gain or out of contempt for authority. They were driven by a desire for representation, freedom, and a more fair and equitable society – principles that were a far cry from the self-serving motivations of most pirates and smugglers. Nonetheless, the shadow of piracy and smuggling looms over the era, a subtle but pervasive reminder of the complex dynamics at play in the birth of a nation.

Chapter 11 Quiz:

1. The _________ Acts, which were designed to protect the commercial interests of Britain, led to widespread smuggling in the American colonies.
2. _________, in their resistance to British economic control, are thought to have unintentionally fostered a sense of independence among the American colonies.
3. The 18th century pirates formed their own communities, demonstrating a spirit of _________ and democracy.
4. Some colonial governors were known to provide pirates with _________, effectively endorsing their defiance of British authority.
5. The _________ were an organization that played a significant role in the lead-up to the Revolutionary War, employing tactics similar to pirates and smugglers.
6. The Boston Tea Party, a famous act of defiance leading up to the Revolution, was essentially an act of _________.
7. Revolutionaries were driven by a desire for representation, freedom, and a more fair and _________ society.

Chapter Twelve: The Revolutionary War – Pirates vs. Patriots

The Role of Piracy during the Revolutionary War

The American Revolutionary War, a colossal clash between the thirteen colonies and the British Empire, isn't often associated with pirates. But surprise, surprise! Pirates indeed had a unique part to play in this monumental event. It was during this time that the blurred line between pirates and privateers became even more obscure.

Privateers were similar to pirates, but they sailed under the flag of a nation, operating with that nation's blessing to raid and plunder enemy vessels. During the Revolutionary War, privateering became a preferred method for the colonies to strike back at the British Empire. With a fledgling navy and a lack of resources, the colonists turned to these seafaring opportunists for assistance. Armed with a document known as a "Letter of Marque," colonial privateers became sanctioned pirates.

Privateering offered a way for the newly formed United States to wage a kind of economic warfare against Britain. They could attack British trade, disrupt their supply lines, and even seize much-needed supplies for the colonial cause. The colonists' endorsement of privateering was essentially a legal loophole that allowed piracy to flourish, all in the name of freedom and independence.

In terms of the economy, these privateers brought in a significant amount of wealth to the colonies. The spoils taken from British ships - everything from armaments to food to luxury goods - were sold off, and the profits often funneled back into the colonial war effort. As the war dragged on, the privateers proved instrumental in sustaining the fight against the British Empire.

Notable Incidents Involving Pirates

One of the most dramatic episodes of piracy during the Revolutionary War was the exploits of the privateer ship named "The Defence." Commanded by Captain John Manley, The Defence was known for its daring raids against British vessels. One of the most memorable captures was that of the British ship Nancy in November 1775.

The Nancy was a massive British ordnance ship loaded to the brim with weapons, gunpowder, and other supplies meant for British troops in Boston. Captain Manley, with his uncanny knack for identifying British vessels and his intimate knowledge of the Massachusetts coastline, intercepted the Nancy just as it was nearing its destination.

The capture of the Nancy was a significant blow to the British, but a tremendous boon to the colonists. The haul included over 2,000 muskets, 30,000 round shot, and a treasure trove of gunpowder – all critical supplies that the colonial army desperately needed. The goods taken from the Nancy were later used in the Siege of Boston, contributing to the eventual colonial victory.

Another notable privateer of the Revolutionary War was Captain Gustavus Conyngham, also known as the "Dunkirk Pirate." Conyngham was a particularly thorny issue for the British. Operating out of Dunkirk, France, he and his crew on the "Revenge" successfully intercepted and captured numerous British vessels, disrupting their trade and causing significant financial loss.

The exploits of these privateers, essentially pirates in the eyes of the British, played an undeniable part in the American Revolution. They were risky, daring, and often reckless in their pursuit of enemy vessels. Still, their contributions to the colonial cause helped turn the tide of the war, providing a spark of hope in an otherwise bleak situation. Their adventures serve as a testament to the unconventional tactics that helped forge a new nation.

Chapter 12 Quiz:

    1. The ___________ War was a time when the line between

pirates and privateers became even more obscure.

2. Privateers were similar to pirates, but they sailed under the flag of a __________.

3. Armed with a document known as a "________________," colonial privateers became sanctioned pirates.

4. Privateering offered a way for the newly formed United States to wage a kind of _________ warfare against Britain.

5. The Defence, commanded by Captain __________, was known for its daring raids against British vessels.

6. The capture of the ship __________ was a significant blow to the British, but a tremendous boon to the colonists.

7. The goods taken from the Nancy were later used in the __________ of Boston, contributing to the eventual colonial victory.

8. Captain __________ Conyngham, also known as the "Dunkirk Pirate," was a particularly thorny issue for the British.

Chapter Thirteen: Legacy of Piracy in Colonial America

Examination of the Lasting Impact of Piracy on Colonial America

Piracy has left an indelible mark on the history and development of colonial America. It played a significant role in the economic, political, and social landscapes of the time, impacting the growth of colonies, relationships with European powers, and the evolution of maritime law. Its legacy is so intertwined with the early years of colonial America that it's difficult to discuss one without acknowledging the other.

Trade was a fundamental pillar of colonial life and economic development. Pirates, though often viewed negatively, stimulated economic growth by circulating goods and wealth. The relationship between pirates and colonial settlements was symbiotic. Pirates provided the colonists with much-needed goods and currencies, particularly during periods of trade restrictions imposed by European powers, while the colonists offered pirates safe harbors, a market for their loot, and a place to recruit crew members.

Pirates also served as a form of indirect resistance against the oppressive policies of European powers. They became the embodiment of rebellion and freedom, defying the conventional norms and restrictions of their era. Their actions challenged the monopoly of trading companies, disrupted established economic systems, and forced a rethinking of colonial policies and maritime laws.

Despite the negative aspects of piracy, including violence and lawlessness, some pirates were seen as heroes, celebrated in songs, stories, and folklore. Their tales of daring exploits, rebellions against authority, and pursuit of freedom resonated with colonists who desired independence.

The legacy of piracy in colonial America is far more complex and impactful than often recognized. Its influence stretches beyond sea battles and treasure maps to the underpinnings of America's early economic and social structures.

Influence on Maritime Law and International Relations

The prevalence of piracy during the colonial period also had profound effects on maritime law and international relations. European powers, beleaguered by the threats posed by pirates, had to revise their maritime laws and policies. Anti-piracy laws were enacted, and colonial authorities were given more powers to combat piracy. The need to fight against a common enemy also led to rare instances of cooperation between rival powers, laying the groundwork for modern international maritime law.

Moreover, piracy played a role in defining the sovereignty and jurisdiction of nations over the open seas. The issue of who had the right to prosecute pirates was a contentious one, often leading to disputes between nations. These debates contributed to the development of the concept of "universal jurisdiction", which holds that some crimes are so heinous that they can be prosecuted by any nation, regardless of where the crime was committed or the nationality of the perpetrators or victims.

Economic, Social, and Cultural Consequences

Economically, pirates played an influential role in shaping the colonial marketplace. They infused much-needed capital into the colonial economy by introducing foreign currencies and goods. Pirate marketplaces became hives of activity where goods from around the world could be found. They helped to stimulate economic growth and fostered a degree of economic independence.

The social and cultural impact of piracy was equally significant. Pirates were social misfits, individuals who had defied the norms of society to live by their own rules. This defiance was not just an act of rebellion, but also a demonstration of freedom and autonomy, concepts that greatly appealed to the colonists, many of whom were seeking a new life free from the constraints and traditions of their homelands.

Culturally, pirates have been immortalized in American folklore, literature, and popular culture. Their exploits have been romanticized and embellished, giving rise to the image of the swashbuckling rogue, a symbol of rebellion and freedom. From "Treasure Island" to "Pirates of the Caribbean", pirates have been depicted as daring adventurers and anti-heroes, their stories appealing to our fascination with rebellion, freedom, and the thrill of the unknown.

In conclusion, the legacy of piracy in colonial America is a rich and complex tapestry, woven from threads of economic necessity, rebellion against authority, and the quest for freedom. Its impact on the development of colonial America and the evolution of maritime law and international relations cannot be understated. Pirates, for better or worse, have left a lasting mark on American history that continues to influence us today.

Chapter 13 Quiz:

1. Pirates played a significant role in the economic, political, and social landscapes of colonial America, impacting the growth of colonies, relationships with European powers, and the evolution of ____________.
2. Despite the negative aspects of piracy, including violence and lawlessness, some pirates were seen as ____________, celebrated in songs, stories, and folklore.
3. The legacy of piracy in colonial America stretches beyond sea battles and treasure maps to the underpinnings of America's early economic and ____________ structures.
4. Economically, pirates played an influential role in shaping the ____________ marketplace.
5. Pirates became social ____________, individuals who had

defied the norms of society to live by their own rules.

6. The prevalence of piracy during the colonial period also had profound effects on ______________ and international relations.

7. The issue of who had the right to prosecute pirates was a contentious one, often leading to disputes between nations. These debates contributed to the development of the concept of ______________.

Chapter Fourteen: Pirate Legends and Folklore

Exploration of Myths, Legends & Popular Culture Surrounding Pirates

Despite their often grim reality, pirates have been romanticized and immortalized in stories and myths, becoming a potent symbol in popular culture. Published in Britain in 1724, "A General History of the Robberies and Murders of the Most Notorious Pyrates" by Captain Charles Johnson contains biographies of pirates from the time in which it was written and had a significant impact on how people conceptualized pirates until this day. The book serves as the primary source for the lives of many famous pirates, giving the most colorful personalities near mythological status. It is also possible that the author made up a lot of what he wrote about pirates.

The book was very successful in its time. It catered to the desire for the exotic among the British audience, who delighted in violent tales of piracy. "It has been said, and there seems no reason to question this, that Captain Johnson created the modern conception of pirates," says English naval historian David Cordingly.

In the early years of piracy, tales of fearsome and ruthless men, navigating the high seas, seeking treasure and adventure, began to circulate. These stories painted a portrait of pirates as swashbuckling rogues, living by their wits in a world ruled by the law of the sword. They were pictured with distinctive clothing and accessories like tricorn hats, eyepatches, and parrots. However, not all of these are historically accurate. For instance, eyepatches were not a common accessory.

The legends of buried treasure are also a significant part of pirate mythology, popularized by works such as Robert Louis Stevenson's "Treasure Island". Yet, in reality, burying treasure was not a common practice among pirates. The notorious pirate William Kidd is one of the few known to have buried his loot.

Perhaps the most pervasive myth is that of the pirate dialect. Our perception of pirate speech, filled with "arrrs" and "mateys," can be traced back largely to Robert Newton's portrayal of Long John Silver in the 1950 film adaptation of "Treasure Island." However, there's no historical evidence that pirates spoke in a unique dialect.

One true element in the folklore is the Jolly Roger - the skull and crossbones flag. Many pirate crews did use such symbols, although the designs varied widely, with some featuring hearts, hourglasses, or whole skeletons.

The Influence of Literature and Media on Pirate Imagery

The image of pirates we have today is greatly influenced by literature and media. The aforementioned "Treasure Island" painted an enduring portrait of pirates and their lifestyle. Another influential work was "Pirates of the Caribbean", both the Disneyland ride and the later film series. The movies, in particular, were responsible for reviving interest in pirate lore in the 21st century.

In literature, the character of the pirate has often been used to explore themes of freedom, rebellion, and the human spirit. This is evident in works like "Pirate Latitudes" by Michael Crichton and "Sea Queens: Women Pirates Around the World" by Jane Yolen, which offer alternative perspectives on the pirate narrative.

In films and television, pirates are typically portrayed as charismatic antiheroes. They are often shown to possess a certain honor code and show kindness to those in need, contrasting with their criminal activities. This dichotomy adds depth to their characters and makes them more appealing to audiences.

Chapter 14 Quiz:

1. Despite their often grim reality, pirates have been _________________ and immortalized in stories and myths, becoming a potent symbol in popular culture.
2. The notorious pirate _____________ is one of the few known to have buried his loot.
3. The image of pirates we have today is greatly influenced by

literature and media such as ______________ and "Pirates of the Caribbean."

Conclusion: Echoes from the Age of Sails, Swords, and Smugglers

What a thrilling adventure we've been on! From the rumbling decks of pirate galleons to secret smuggler hideouts, we've journeyed through the shadows and echoes of colonial America. We've met fearsome pirates and daring smugglers, brave colonial folk and powerful monarchs, as they navigated an era bristling with change.

In the beginning, we set sail into the past, tracing the routes of spice traders and treasure fleets. We learned why these precious goods made the New World such an attractive place for everyone - including pirates and smugglers. Can you still remember the intoxicating scent of exotic spices and the gleam of pirate gold?

Then we journeyed to the American colonies, exploring the intriguing and complex relationship they had with pirates and smugglers. From Rhode Island to North Carolina, these colonies were both victims and beneficiaries of pirate activities.

We sailed across the Atlantic to Europe, the heart of colonial power. The rivalries between Spain, England, France, Portugal, and the Netherlands fueled piracy, making the seas a chess-board of power and wealth. Do you recall how the waters of the Caribbean turned into a Pirate's Paradise, and the unwitting role Africa played in this dangerous game?

Our voyage then took us into the Golden Age of Piracy. We met pirates whose names are now the stuff of legends - Blackbeard, Calico Jack, Anne Bonny, and Mary Read. Their deeds, both terrible and extraordinary, have left an indelible mark on history.

Then we witnessed how the Revolutionary War gave a new face to pirates and smugglers. From foes to friends, their roles shifted as the 13 colonies battled for independence. We saw how the war efforts could not have been possible without the covert help of those who knew the seas best.

The sun began to set on our journey as we explored the fall of piracy and smuggling. Through concerted efforts by naval forces and colonial authorities, pirates and smugglers were gradually brought to justice, and peace once again returned to the seas.

As our journey neared its end, we looked at the enduring spirit of piracy, its influence on the rebellion, and its echoes in legends and folklore. Finally, we examined the profound legacy of piracy on colonial America, which shaped not just economic, social, and cultural landscapes, but also maritime law and international relations.

Now, as we drop anchor and step ashore, we can look back

at our voyage and realize that the echoes of this exciting era still reverberate in the modern world. From the establishment of maritime laws to the spirit of rebellion, the age of pirates and smugglers has significantly shaped the world we know today. The stories of their daring exploits continue to captivate our imagination, and their legacy, albeit complex, remains an integral part of our shared history.

So, as we leave the decks of the pirate ships and step back into our own world, remember this: the echoes of the Age of Sails, Swords, and Smugglers continue to ripple through our lives. Their adventures may belong to the past, but their influence lives on. Our voyage may be over, but the stories of piracy and smuggling in colonial America continue to unfold, challenging us to learn more, explore further, and appreciate the nuances of our vibrant past.

If you've enjoyed this book, please leave a 5-star review on Amazon because it will help other students find it. Also, follow me on Amazon to see other books you might like.

Discussion/Essay questions to get you thinking about what you've read...

1. Why were the European countries interested in establishing colonies in the New World? What were some of the goods they were particularly interested in?

2. Describe the role of pirates during the colonial era. How did they impact the societies and economies of the colonies?

3. What was the "Golden Age of Piracy"? Who were some of the famous pirates from this era?

4. How did the colonial authorities and naval forces work together to bring an end to piracy? Give examples of some strategies they used.

5. How did smuggling contribute to the colonial economy? Why was it considered necessary by some colonists?

6. How did the rivalry between Spain and England fuel piracy and smuggling in the colonial era? Provide examples from the text.

7. Discuss the relationship between piracy and the spirit of independence. How might the defiance of authority by pirates and smugglers have influenced the revolutionaries?

8. How did piracy and smuggling influence maritime law and international relations?

9. What role did Africa play in the colonial era? How did the triangular trade and the Middle Passage affect Africa and its people?

10. Who were the Taino and Carib peoples? How did European colonization impact their societies and cultures?

11. What was the "Pirate Round"? How did it contribute to the wealth and success of pirates during the colonial era?

12. Discuss the role of pirates and smugglers during the Revolutionary War. How did their activities support the war efforts?

13. Describe the relationship between the 13 American colonies and the British Caribbean colonies. How did piracy and smuggling influence this relationship?

14. What are some myths and legends surrounding pirates? How have literature and media influenced our perception of pirates?

15. How has the legacy of piracy in colonial America shaped modern society, culture, and law?

16. What are some of the daring high-seas robberies and fierce battles between pirates sand the British Navy? How did these events shape the history of colonial America?

17. Who were some of the most prominent pirate hunters of the colonial era? What strategies did they use to capture or

eliminate pirates?

18. Discuss the lasting impacts of the era of sails, swords, and smugglers on the modern world.

19. How has the history of piracy in colonial America been represented in popular culture? Do you think these representations are accurate or exaggerated?

20. If you were living in the colonial era, would you view pirates as villains or heroes? Justify your answer with examples from the text.

PIRATE MAPS

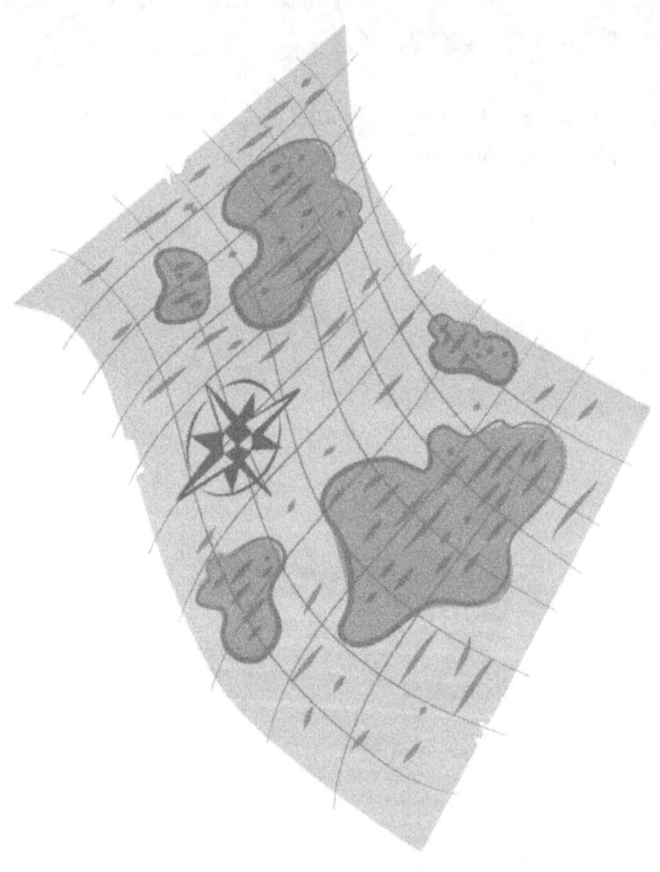

Pirate Maps

Check out these maps to learn more about the locations mentioned in this book. You can see what the places look like now. Hopefully, they'll also give you ideas for your own pirate stories that you can write in the next section.

The "Pirate Round" started in the Caribbean, known for its bustling ports and pirate havens, then stretched thousands of miles east, around the southern tip of Africa, and into the Indian Ocean, before looping back to the Caribbean and up to the 13 American colonies. See the Google map at https://bit.ly/PirateRound.

While the romantic notion of pirates burying their treasure is largely a myth propelled by literature and pop culture, there have been a few historical accounts and legends suggesting certain locations as the final resting places of pirate wealth. Here are some specific places spanning from the Caribbean to Massachusetts that are associated with stories of buried pirate treasure, as well as other hot spots in colonial America and the Caribbean during the Golden Age of Piracy mentioned in my book.

Remember, some of these are largely legends and tales that have been passed down through generations. While they capture our imagination, attempts to find these treasures have often resulted in disappointment. The real treasure of these tales is their ability to connect us with a past era of exploration, adventure, and maritime mystery. See the Google map at https://bit.ly/Pirate-Map.

Pirate Story Writing Prompts

Do you like to write stories?

I wrote a book called Imagination Station to teach kids the basics of short story writing. You can check it out at https://amzn.to/3qDBiLN. For now, practice writing fun pirate stories with these story starters.

Below are 20 creative writing prompts to stimulate your imagination. Write short stories based on these prompts…

1. Write a story about a young pirate experiencing their first sea battle during the Golden Age of Piracy.

2. You are a colonist in New England and your town has just been visited by a pirate ship. Write a story about the interaction between the pirates and the townsfolk.

3. Imagine you are a cabin boy or girl on a ship that was just captured by the infamous pirate Blackbeard. Describe your experience.

4. Write a story about an unlikely friendship between a European privateer and a Taino warrior during the colonial era.

5. Imagine you're living in the 18th century Caribbean and you stumble upon a pirate's hidden treasure. What happens next?

6. Create a story based on a fabled encounter between the feared pirate Anne Bonny and a British Navy Captain.

7. Write a tale about a secret network of smugglers in the North American colonies.

8. You're a pirate who decided to retire and hide your life of piracy. Write a story about your new life and the challenges you face in keeping your past a secret.

9. Imagine you're a merchant in colonial America, struggling with the moral implications of buying goods from pirates.

10. Write a story about a daring escape from a pirate ship by a captive African during the triangular trade.

11. Create a tale where you are a privateer, hired by one of the European powers during their conflicts. Describe your thrilling adventures.

12. You're a famous pirate hunter. Write about your most challenging mission.

13. Write a story based on the adventures of a young pirate sailing on the "Pirate Round."

14. Imagine you're a colonist witnessing the decline of piracy. Describe how it affects your colony and your personal life.

15. Write a story from the perspective of a pirate living through the end of the Golden Age of Piracy.

16. You're a colonial governor secretly supporting piracy. Describe a situation where your secret almost gets revealed.

17. Write a story about a young girl or boy who runs away from home to join a pirate crew.

18. Imagine you're a sailor on a pirate hunting ship chasing the infamous pirate Calico Jack.

19. Write a story about a former pirate adjusting to a new life after the King's Pardon.

20. You are a pirate who decides to become a patriot during the Revolutionary War. Tell the story of your transformation.

Glossary

Piracy: The act of attacking and robbing ships at sea.

Privateer: A private person or ship authorized by a government during wartime to attack and capture enemy vessels.

Smuggling: The illegal transport of goods or people, such as out of a building, into a prison, or across an international border, in violation of applicable laws or other regulations.

Triangular Trade: The transatlantic trading system between Europe, Africa, and the Americas during the colonial period. Goods were traded from Europe to Africa, enslaved people from Africa to the Americas, and colonial goods from the Americas back to Europe.

Golden Age of Piracy: A period in the early 18th century, roughly spanning the years between 1690 and 1720, considered to be the height of pirate activity in the Caribbean and the Atlantic.

Letter of Marque: A government license authorizing a person (known as a privateer) to attack and capture enemy vessels.

Colony: A country or area under the full or partial political control of another country and occupied by settlers from that country.

Pirate Round: A sailing route followed by certain mainly English pirates, during the late 17th century and early 18th century.

Maroon Communities: Communities formed by escaped enslaved people, often in remote areas.

The Middle Passage: The sea journey undertaken by slave ships from West Africa to the West Indies during the Atlantic Slave Trade.

Buccaneer: A pirate, especially one who preyed on Spanish shipping in the West Indies during the 17th century.

Mutiny: An open rebellion against the proper authorities, especially by soldiers or sailors against their officers.

Galleon: A large three-masted sailing ship with a square rig and usually two or more decks, used from the 15th to the 17th century.

Jolly Roger: The traditional English name for the flags flown to identify a pirate ship about to attack, during the early 18th century.

Doubloons: Gold coins formerly used in Spain and Spanish America.

Pieces of Eight: A Spanish silver coin, originally worth eight reales; later, it became the model for the American dollar.

Naval Blockade: An effort to cut off supplies, war material, or communications from a particular area by force, usually via sea.

Press-gang: A group of people, historically naval officers, who would force men into service, often naval service, by coercive techniques.

Black Market: An illegal traffic or trade in officially controlled or scarce commodities.

Cartography: The science or practice of drawing maps.

Pirate Jokes & Songs

As you've learned, the pirates of old have had a lasting effect on popular culture. Here are some pirate jokes, as well as pirate songs, aka "sea shanties."

20 pirate jokes:

1. Why did nobody want to play cards with the pirate?
   Because he was standing on the deck.

2. How do pirates prefer to communicate?
   Aye to aye!

3. What's a pirate's favorite letter?
   Ye think it be "R", but a pirate's true love be the "C" (sea).

4. Why are pirates so mean?
   They just arrrrrr!

5. What did the sea say to the pirate?
   Nothing, it just waved.

6. Why did the pirate go on vacation?
   He needed some arrrrrr and arrrrrr!

7. How do you save a pirate from drowning?
   Take your foot off his head!

8. What has 8 legs, 8 arms, and 8 eyes?
   8 pirates!

9. What's a pirate's favorite part of a song?
   The hook!

10. What do you call a pirate with two eyes and two legs?
   A rookie.

11. Why did the pirate become a baker?
   Because he found his true "roll".

12. Why do pirates never use a smartphone?
   They can't find the 'X' to close the ads!

13. Why don't pirates shower before they walk the plank?
   Because they'll just wash up on shore later.

14. How do pirates know that they are pirates?
   They think, therefore they ARRR!

15. What do you call a pirate with a cat?
   Purrr-ate!

16. How do you call a pirate that skips class?
   Captain Hooky!

17. Why couldn't the pirate play cards?
   Because he was sitting on the deck.

18. What's a pirate's favorite country?

ARRRgentina!

19. What did the pirate say on his 80th birthday?
   Aye matey (I'm eighty)!

20. What's orange and sounds like a parrot?
   A carrot!

And here are the lyrics for 3 popular sea shanties:

Blow the Man Down
   Oh, blow the man down, bullies, blow the man down
   To me way-aye, blow the man down
   Blow the man down, bullies, blow him away
   Give me some time to blow the man down

Drunken Sailor
   What shall we do with a drunken sailor?
   What shall we do with a drunken sailor?
   What shall we do with a drunken sailor?
   Early in the morning?

Way hay and up she rises
   Way hay and up she rises
   Way hay and up she rises
   Early in the morning

Yo Ho (A Pirate's Life for Me)
   Yo ho, yo ho, a pirate's life for me.
   We pillage plunder, we rifle and loot.

Drink up me 'earties, yo ho.
We kidnap and ravage and don't give a hoot.
Drink up me 'earties, yo ho.

Yo ho, yo ho, a pirate's life for me.
We extort and pilfer, we filch and sack.
Drink up me 'earties, yo ho.
Maraud and embezzle and even highjack.
Drink up me 'earties, yo ho.

Yo ho, yo ho, a pirate's life for me.
We kindle and char and in flame and ignite.
Drink up me 'earties, yo ho.
We burn up the city, we're really a fright.
Drink up me 'earties, yo ho.

We're rascals and scoundrels, we're villains and knaves.
Drink up me 'earties, yo ho.
We're devils and black sheep, we're really bad eggs.
Drink up me 'earties, yo ho.

Yo ho, yo ho, a pirate's life for me.
We're beggars and blighters and ne'er do-well cads,
Drink up me 'earties, yo ho.
Aye, but we're loved by our mommies and dads,
Drink up me 'earties, yo ho.

Bibliography

1. "Under the Black Flag: The Romance and the Reality of Life Among the Pirates." David Cordingly. Random House, 1996.

2. "Pirate Hunter of the Caribbean: The Adventurous Life of Captain Woodes Rogers." David Cordingly. Random House, 2011.

3. "Pirates: The Golden Age of Piracy: A History From Beginning to End." Hourly History, 2016.

4. "The Pirate's Pact: The Secret Alliances Between History's Most Notorious Buccaneers and Colonial America." Douglas R. Burgess. McGraw Hill, 2008.

5. "Blackbeard: America's Most Notorious Pirate." Angus Konstam. Wiley, 2006.

6. "Colonial America: A History to 1763." Richard Middleton and Anne Lombard. Wiley-Blackwell, 2011.

7. "Sea Queens: Women Pirates Around the World." Jane Yolen. Charlesbridge, 2008.

8. "If a Pirate I Must Be...: The True Story of "Black Bart," King of the Caribbean Pirates." Richard Sanders. Skyhorse, 2007.

9. "Pirates in Their Own Words." E.T. Fox. Fox Historical, 2014.

10. "The Many-Headed Hydra: Sailors, Slaves, Commoners,

and the Hidden History of the Revolutionary Atlantic." Peter Linebaugh and Marcus Rediker. Beacon Press, 2000.

11. "The Republic of Pirates: Being the True and Surprising Story of the Caribbean Pirates and the Man Who Brought Them Down." Colin Woodard. Houghton Mifflin Harcourt, 2008.